The Ultimate Plant Based Diet

Your Comprehensive Guide to Sustainable and Delicious Plant-Powered Living, with Budget-Friendly Meals for a Healthy Vegan Lifestyle

Lane Payne

The Ultimate Plant Based Diet
© Copyright 2023 by Lane Payne
All rights reserved

This document is geared towards providing exact and reliable information with regards to the topic and issue covered. The publication is sold with the idea that the publisher is not required to render accounting, officially permitted, or otherwise, qualified services. If advice is necessary, legal or professional, a practiced individual in the profession should be ordered. From a Declaration of Principles which was accepted and approved equally by a Committee of the American Bar Association and a Committee of Publishers and Associations. In no way is it legal to reproduce, duplicate, or transmit any part of this document in either electronic means or in printed format. Recording of this publication is strictly prohibited and any storage of this document is not allowed unless with written permission from the publisher.

All rights reserved.

The information provided herein is stated to be truthful and consistent, in that any liability, in terms of inattention or otherwise, by any usage or abuse of any policies, processes, or directions contained within is the solitary and utter responsibility of the recipient reader. Under no circumstances will any legal responsibility or blame be held against the publisher for any reparation, damages, or monetary loss due to the information herein, either directly or indirectly. Respective authors own all copyrights not held by the publisher. The information herein is offered for informational purposes solely, and is universal as so. The presentation of the information is without contract or any type of guarantee assurance. The trademarks that are used are without any consent, and the publication of the trademark is without permission or backing by the trademark owner. All trademarks and brands within this book are for clarifying purposes only and are the owned by the owners themselves, not affiliated with this document.

TABLE OF CONTENTS

CHAPTER 1: INTRODUCING THE PLANT-BASED LIFESTYLE 1

The Rise of Plant-Powered Living 1

The Health Benefits of a Plant-Based Diet 3

Environmental Impact of Plant-Based Eating 6

Debunking Myths about Veganism 8

Your Journey to a Vegan Lifestyle 10

CHAPTER 2: UNDERSTANDING PLANT-BASED NUTRITION 15

The Basics of Nutrition 15

Protein and the Plant-Based Diet 17

Essential Vitamins and Minerals in a Vegan Diet 20

Balancing Macronutrients for Optimal Health 22

Addressing Nutritional Concerns in Veganism 24

CHAPTER 3: TRANSITIONING TO A PLANT-BASED DIET 27

Preparing Your Kitchen 27

Plants You Should Start Loving 29

Gradual Transition vs. Overnight Change 31

Dealing with Cravings 33

Setting Yourself Up for Success 35

CHAPTER 4: PLANNING YOUR PLANT-BASED DIET 39

Understanding Your Caloric Needs 39

Creating a Balanced Plate 41

Weekly Meal Planning 101 43

The Art of Mindful Eating 45

Tips for Grocery Shopping on a Budget 47

CHAPTER 5: QUICK AND EASY PLANT-BASED BREAKFAST RECIPES 51

Green Smoothie Magic 51

High-Protein Vegan Pancakes 53

Overnight Oats Variations 55

Tofu Scramble and Vegan "Eggs" 57

Power-Packed Breakfast Bowls 59

CHAPTER 6: SATISFYING PLANT-BASED LUNCHES 63

Buddha Bowl Basics 63

Vegan Sandwiches and Wraps 65

Plant-Based Pasta Dishes 67

Hearty Vegan Salads 69

Quick and Easy Soups 71

CHAPTER 7: DELICIOUS PLANT-BASED DINNERS 73

Vegan Pizza and Flatbreads 73

Plant-Powered Stir Frys 75

Comforting Vegan Casseroles 76

Vegan Burger Variations 78

One-Pot Wonders 80

CHAPTER 8: SNACKS AND DESSERTS 83

Healthy Vegan Snacks for On the Go 83

Energy Balls and Bars 85

Guilt-Free Vegan Desserts 86

Smoothie Bowl Creations 88

Plant-Based Baking Basics 90

BONUS 1: AUDIOBOOK 93

BONUS 2: VIDEO 95

EXCLUSIVE BONUS: 3 EBOOK 97

AUTHOR BIO: LANE PAYNE 99

Lane Payne

CHAPTER 1

INTRODUCING THE PLANT-BASED LIFESTYLE

The Rise of Plant-Powered Living

The popularity of plant-based diets has steadily grown over the past decade, with more and more people opting to eliminate or reduce animal products for health, ethical, environmental, and other reasons. This shift represents an exciting movement towards more sustainable and compassionate living.

Several factors have contributed to the rising adoption of plant-forward lifestyles. One is the greater awareness of the impacts of animal agriculture on issues like climate change, pollution, deforestation, and antibiotic resistance. For example, the FAO estimates livestock production generates 14.5% of human-induced greenhouse gas emissions globally. As more consumers learn about this connection, many feel motivated to align their diets with their eco-conscious values.

In addition, films like Food, Inc. and books like The China Study have exposed some of the concerning practices used in factory farming and linked animal product consumption to diseases like cancer and heart disease. With this amplified visibility, many have decided to go vegan or vegetarian out of concern for animal welfare or to reduce health risks.

The market has responded to this demand by expanding plant-based offerings exponentially. Data shows sales of plant-based foods grew 20% in 2020 alone, far exceeding the rate of total food sales. This growth has made following a vegan diet more convenient than ever before. Mainstream restaurants like Burger King now serve meatless burgers, and plant-based dairy and meat alternatives line grocery store shelves. The accessibility makes plant-based choices easy.

Social media and the internet have also allowed the vegan community to flourish by sharing recipes and advice. Connecting with like-minded people provides information and accountability. Seeing the vibrant vegan lifestyle portrayed online helps eliminate fears of restriction or deprivation.

Cultural shifts have also facilitated the change. Being vegan or vegetarian used to be seen as abnormal, but it is now considered mainstream. Celebrities, athletes, and public figures proudly adopting plant-based eating have inspired fans to make the switch and reduced the stigma. Younger generations in particular have embraced flexitarian, vegetarian, and vegan diets as part of their identity.

Of course, interest in the benefits of plants themselves has also bolstered the movement. From colorful fruits and vegetables to ancient grains, nuts, seeds, and legumes, the incredible array of nutritious and satisfying plant foods available makes going plant-based easy and enjoyable. Spinach and kale provide iron, berries deliver antioxidants, avocados offer healthy fats - the list goes on. Appreciating plants' nutritional qualities has been central to the trend.

The appeal also goes beyond health. For many, it is an exciting culinary adventure to experience all the possibilities of plant-based cuisine. From hearty mushroom bourguignon to creamy cauliflower Alfredo, the options are endless. Online communities and cookbooks provide ample recipes to create delicious, satisfying meals free of animal products.

This extends to plant-based meat and dairy substitutes which have achieved new levels of quality, taste, and texture. Options like almond milk, seitan "wings", and cashew cheese make eliminating animal products seamless and approachable. Those transitioning to veganism are often pleasantly surprised by the array of choices available.

Of course, the plant-powered movement still faces challenges. Misconceptions about vegan diets lacking key nutrients like protein and iron persist. The need for supplementation or fortified foods to achieve optimal health on an exclusively plant diet continues to be debated. Social hurdles around family meals and dining out also remain.

However, the momentum only continues to build as more resources and support systems emerge to facilitate the transition. From doctors to dietitians, many health professionals now enthusiastically endorse and even recommend plant-forward eating. And compassionate, patient advocates provide helpful guidance to the newly veg-curious in a constructive way.

This welcoming, inclusive atmosphere helps sustain lasting change. Each person's journey will be unique, but the broader community is there to encourage taking steps towards more ethical, environmentally-friendly, and health-promoting plant-based eating - whether it's Meatless Mondays, or going vegan overnight.

In many ways, the rise of plant-powered living signifies shifting attitudes and increased consciousness around our own health, animals, and the planet. What started as a fringe movement has entered the mainstream, promising to change consumption and habits for the better. The coming decades will show how far this momentum can go towards creating a more sustainable food system and society.

The Health Benefits of a Plant-Based Diet

A whole foods, plant-based diet offers tremendous benefits for long-term health and wellbeing. By focusing on natural, minimally processed plant foods, we can prevent, treat, and often reverse many common chronic diseases.

Research consistently shows that a diet centered on fruits, vegetables, whole grains, legumes, nuts and seeds protects against heart disease, Type 2 diabetes, obesity, cancer, and cognitive decline. The fiber, nutrients, antioxidants and phytochemicals in plants work synergistically to optimize our health in ways that animal products can't match.

One of the most well-documented effects is cardiovascular protection. Plant-based diets have been shown to prevent and reverse heart disease by lowering cholesterol, blood pressure, and inflammation. The fiber helps remove plaque buildup in arteries. Vegan diets reduce heart disease mortality by up to 19% compared to omnivore diets.

Type 2 diabetes is a modern epidemic directly linked to lifestyle factors like diet. Whole plant foods help regulate blood sugar levels and insulin sensitivity due to their fiber content and complex carbs. Those eating vegan and vegetarian diets have just half the rates of diabetes seen in meat eaters. Plant-based diets can also improve diabetic neuropathy, retinopathy, and nephropathy.

Excess weight and obesity are major risk factors for many chronic illnesses. Focusing on unrefined, high-volume plant foods makes it easier to manage a healthy weight. Vegans tend to have lower BMI levels compared to both vegetarians and meat eaters. One reason is fiber's ability to promote satiety. The thermic effect of food, which is the energy required to process nutrients, is also higher for plant versus animal foods.

There is extensive evidence linking regular meat consumption to increased cancer risk. Processed meats are classified as carcinogenic by the World Health Organization. Plants contain a spectrum of cancer-protective compounds. Cruciferous vegetables, berries, garlic, mushrooms and green tea are especially potent for suppressing tumor growth. Those adhering to plant-based diets experience 22% lower cancer rates.

Brain health also benefits from a predominance of healthy plant foods. The risk of developing Alzheimer's and dementia is markedly decreased for vegans and vegetarians compared to omnivores. Omega-3 fatty acids from microalgae, nuts, seeds and leafy greens support cognitive function. Polyphenols and antioxidants in plants protect against neuronal damage that leads to cognitive decline.

In additional to disease prevention, plant-based diets are linked to lower all-cause mortality rates. One extensive study following over 130,000 people for 18 years found pescatarians, vegetarians, and vegans had 12%, 19%, and 15% lower mortality respectively compared to meat eaters. Not only do plant-focused diets extend lifespan, but they boost quality of life through healthier aging.

Some nutrients of particular importance on a vegan diet include vitamin B12, vitamin D, iron, zinc, iodine, EPA/DHA and protein. Through careful meal planning and strategic use of fortified foods or supplements where needed, it is easy to obtain optimal intake of these nutrients. Variety is key to prevent potential shortfalls.

Focusing your diet on whole plant foods naturally helps achieve ideal weight while flooding your body with disease-fighting antioxidants, anti-inflammatory compounds, and protective phytonutrients. Plants offer a powerhouse of vitamins, minerals, fiber and healthy carbohydrates, protein, essential fats and more. A nutritionally balanced plant-based diet provides fuel for both body and mind while optimizing long-term wellness.

The effects of diet choices ripple through families, communities, and society as a whole via healthcare costs, productivity and workforce health. Widespread adoption of plant-based eating has the potential to prevent millions of premature deaths related to chronic, lifestyle-driven diseases. Individuals adhering to predominantly plant-based diets experience better health parameters including:

- Lower blood pressure and resting heart rate.
- Lower LDL and total cholesterol levels.
- Lower rates of heart disease, stroke and Type 2 diabetes.
- Lower cancer risk and increased cancer survival rates.

- Lower BMI and healthier body weight.
- Reduced inflammation and oxidative stress.
- Increased plasma carotenoids and antioxidants.
- Improved insulin sensitivity and blood sugar regulation.
- Enhanced immune function.
- Increased longevity and healthier aging.

A whole foods plant-based diet is profoundly beneficial for both personal health and public health outcomes. While further research is still needed, the existing body of epidemiologic, case control and interventional studies make the advantages clear. The convergence of evidence points to plants as the most health-promoting foods we can eat.

Environmental Impact of Plant-Based Eating

The food we eat has an enormous impact on our planet. Industrial agriculture and factory farming are major contributors to climate change, pollution, habitat destruction, and loss of biodiversity. By switching to a plant-based diet, we can significantly reduce our environmental footprint.

The meat and dairy industries are incredibly resource-intensive. Raising livestock accounts for nearly 15% of global greenhouse gas emissions. Cows produce methane, a potent greenhouse gas, while their manure releases nitrous oxide. The deforestation to create land for grazing and growing feed crops also fuels climate change. Animal agriculture uses nearly 80% of agricultural land yet produces just 18% of the world's calories.

A plant-based diet has a much lower carbon footprint. Production of meat and dairy emits 20-100 times more greenhouse gases per calorie than fruits, vegetables, grains, and legumes. If everyone ate a plant-based diet, studies show we could reduce agricultural land use by 75% while still feeding the global population. This would free up vast amounts of land for natural ecosystems to regenerate.

The meat industry also places a disproportionate burden on water and energy resources. Producing just one hamburger requires 660 gallons of water. It takes 990 gallons of water to produce a gallon of cow's milk. Animal ag is responsible for 24% of water used for agriculture despite providing just 5% of calories consumed. Plant foods have a vastly reduced water footprint. For example, only 22 gallons of water are needed for 1lb of tomatoes.

Factory farms generate huge volumes of waste, much of which ends up polluting our air and waterways. The manure lagoons on these farms emit toxic gases including methane, ammonia, and hydrogen sulfide. Manure runoff enters water systems, causing algal blooms that choke out aquatic life. Animal waste releases gases, pathogens, pharmaceuticals, and excess nutrients. Plant-based agriculture eliminates these major pollution risks.

The expansion of pastures and cropland for animal feed is the primary driver of deforestation, especially in delicate ecosystems like the Amazon. Currently, over 60% of global biodiversity loss is attributed to meat consumption. Clearcutting forests to create pasture land destroys vital habitat for thousands of species. Many are being pushed to extinction.

Switching to plant-based eating would allow forests and wild areas to be preserved. One study found that if everyone in the world shifted to a plant-based diet, the global farmland footprint could be reduced by 75%, freeing up vast amounts of land to support biodiversity.

Eating lower on the food chain conserves resources all along the production chain. It takes much fewer resources to produce nutrient-dense plant foods versus resource-intensive animal products. Given the strain on our natural resources, a global shift toward plant-based eating is critical for environmental sustainability.

As consumers, the easiest way to minimize our environmental impact is to adopt a whole foods, plant-based diet. Focusing on unprocessed fruits, vegetables, grains, nuts, seeds, and legumes tremendously reduces your food-related carbon and water footprint. You'll also be reducing pollution, preserving wild habitat and species, and saving precious resources for future generations.

Even just reducing your consumption of animal products can make a meaningful difference. Consider participating in events like Meatless Mondays to help the environment. Support brands that utilize regenerative agriculture practices. Get involved with environmental organizations lobbying for agricultural reform. Every bite of food we eat has consequences. As stewards of this planet, we have the responsibility to make choices that nurture the earth rather than destroy it. Our collective power as consumers can spark positive change.

Debunking Myths about Veganism

Despite its growth, veganism is still plagued by many myths and misconceptions. Clearing up this disinformation is key to helping more people understand the benefits of plant-based living without irrational fears.

One of the biggest myths is that cutting out all animal products requires dietary deprivation and restriction. In reality, vegan dishes can be just as flavorful, varied, and satisfying as non-vegan cuisine. Creativity with spices, sauces, herbs, veggies, grains and plant-based proteins can produce incredible meals. From enchiladas to burgers, curries to pizzas, the possibilities are infinite. No food group needs to be eliminated.

Related to this, many wrongly assume that veganism lacks key nutrients like protein, iron, calcium and certain vitamins. However, vegetables, fruits, beans, lentils, nuts, seeds and whole grains actually contain an abundance of these essentials. For instance, broccoli has more protein per calorie than steak. Pairing these plant foods thoughtfully provides well-rounded nutrition without meat, eggs or dairy. Those concerned can supplement with vegan-friendly options.

Another myth alleges that vegan diets make you weak. However, many successful plant-powered athletes from tennis champion Venus Williams to boxer David Haye to strongman Patrik Baboumian thrive without animal products. As long as calories and protein needs are met, veganism will not hinder fitness goals. In fact, the fiber and phytonutrients in plants may aid performance. Weight lifters, runners, and pros in almost every sport have excelled on plant-based eating.

Critics also claim veganism is not sustainable long-term, alleging that deprivation or deficiencies will inevitably cause reversion back to meat consumption. However, balanced vegan diets are perfectly healthy over a lifetime. The Academy of Nutrition and Dietetics affirms veganism is suitable for all ages. Millions stick with the lifestyle for good, feeling energized and healthy year after year. With proper eating, veganism is a sustainable choice.

Along the same lines, some argue that veganism is too complicated, requiring extensive planning and knowledge to execute correctly. In certain cases like pregnancy, some extra attention is prudent. But armed with just basic nutrition information, most people can adopt veganism safely. Many foods like beans, tofu, nuts, seeds, and whole grains are simple and nutrient-dense. A bit of meal planning helps, but it does not need to be onerous. Support is widely available to make the transition smooth.

Some critics contend veganism is only for the privileged elite due to the higher cost of certain plant-based specialty items. While exotic superfoods and meat alternatives can be pricey, sticking to basics like produce, beans, and grains generally costs less than buying meat and dairy. Clever shopping and meal prepping keeps costs down too. Beyond economics, though, the desire to prevent animal suffering extends across ethnicities, backgrounds, and classes.

Others argue veganism is a radical, extreme movement. However, a desire to live and eat more kindly without harming animals hardly seems extreme. At its core, veganism simply entails having compassion towards all living beings. Far from being fringe, this principle aligns with many cultural and religious traditions. And cutting out meat, dairy and eggs gradually can be a moderate path.

Some skeptics allege that the health risks of meat and dairy are overblown, dismissing studies linking them to disease. They contend that lean meats and low-fat dairy provide needed nutrients. However, a mountain of research connects even modest amounts of animal foods to higher chances of illness. Plant-based eating allows cutting out that hazard to maximize wellbeing. For those who prioritize health, the evidence strongly favors vegan fare.

Finally, some mythologize veganism itself, assuming those who practice it fit a certain archetype like being militant, judgmental, or passive. In reality, vegans have diverse personalities and advocacy styles. Many tread lightly to create positive change. What unites them is simply caring enough to align habits with values by avoiding animal cruelty. That moral motivation matters more than any label.

Changing misconceptions will take time. But clarifying the true nature of vegan living will allow its principles to spread. With facts, compassion and patience, these myths can be dismantled to pave the way for a more ethical, sustainable, and humane food system. By debunking fallacies, the vegan movement's full potential to create good can be realized.

Your Journey to a Vegan Lifestyle

Transitioning to veganism is a process that unfolds differently for everyone. While some people decide to switch overnight, others ease into it gradually over weeks or months.

There is no right or wrong way - just discovering what feels like the best fit. But cultivating patience, self-compassion and community support can help smooth the path.

For many, the first steps start with information gathering. Reading books, watching documentaries, and researching online allows learning about how veganism aligns with one's values around animals, the environment, health, or sustainability. This knowledge provides motivation to change habits. It may also spark emotions like grief over animal suffering which can be channeled constructively into activism.

Seeking out reasons to stay committed helps sustain the transition too. Some find inspiration in animal rights thinkers, environmental advocates, or healthy, thriving vegan athletes. Others may connect with cultural or religious teachings that emphasize compassion for all living beings. Keeping the "why" of veganism front and center provides meaning and purpose during challenges.

Assessing current eating habits comes next to identify first steps on the journey. Meatless Mondays or giving up just one non-vegan food like cheese can be a gradual place to start. Flexitarian approaches allow working towards veganism incrementally. Even just incorporating more fruits, vegetables and plant proteins sets the stage for bigger changes.

Experimenting with new foods and recipes helps ease the transition diet-wise. Trying plant-based dairy and egg replacements in familiar dishes can be a non-threatening introduction. Blending some mock meats into plant-forward meals offers an approachable bridge. Letting go of attachments to animal-based foods gradually may feel more comfortable.

However, completely eliminating all animal products overnight works well for some too. Ripping the band-aid off means quickly aligning actions with ideals. Following a ready-made 7-day meal plan, challenge, or online program can provide structure here. Though intense, this path sets change in motion decisively.

Regardless of pace, stumbling blocks will happen: intense cravings, social pressures, travel snafus, feeling restricted. Expecting and accepting imperfection prevents abandonment after slip-ups. Reframing setbacks as learning experiences helps recommit with compassion, not criticism. Each day offers a new opportunity to align choices with values.

Building a support system transforms the journey. Joining online or local groups creates community with like-minded others. Connecting with mentors, reading memoirs, or following inspiring social media accounts generates motivation too. Surrounding oneself with encouragement bolsters resilience. If significant health issues arise, consulting a vegan-friendly doctor, dietitian or nutritionist provides specialized guidance.

Keeping it simple and routine makes vegan living effortless. Identifying go-to meals, staple ingredients, and snacks eliminates decision fatigue. Meal prepping or ordering from vegan eateries simplifies eating out. With delicious, nourishing options on hand for busy days, staying on track becomes second nature.

Above all, self-compassion greases the wheels for long-term change. Beating oneself up over missteps undermines sustainability. Transitioning at one's own pace without inner judgment keeps motivation intact. Each small choice towards more ethical, healthy plant-based eating represents meaningful progress.

The journey's challenges should not obscure the profound joys and community belonging veganism can bring. Following one's conscience feels profoundly fulfilling. The transformation of perspectives, habits and tastes can elicit deep appreciation for plants, animals and nature. With an open heart, the path leads towards a life of purpose.

Of course, there is no single "right" roadmap to adopting veganism. Some paths are winding, others straightforward. Minimalism or maximalism both work. What matters most is forward movement driven by compassion. With patience and support, small steps accumulate into lasting, meaningful change. Wherever one is starting from, the journey holds richness and wonder.

Lane Payne

CHAPTER 2

UNDERSTANDING PLANT-BASED NUTRITION

The Basics of Nutrition

Understanding fundamental nutrition is key to planning a healthy vegan diet. While specific needs vary based on age, gender, and activity level, some guiding principles apply universally. Covering these basics sets the stage for getting balanced nutrition from plant-based eating.

First, macronutrients provide the bulk of calories and energy. Carbohydrates, protein and fat all play crucial roles in the body, so adequately consuming each on a daily basis is important. Complex carbs like whole grains deliver glucose for fuel and brain function. Plant proteins rebuild tissues and muscles while keeping you feeling full. Healthy fats maintain skin health and nutrient absorption too.

Micronutrients including vitamins, minerals and phytochemicals are equally vital. Though needed in smaller amounts, they enable key bodily processes from bone growth to eye function. Variety is the key - different colorful phytonutrient-rich produce items provide a range of essential vitamins and minerals.

Calories provide a measure of energy content in foods which must be balanced with activity levels to maintain healthy weight. While nutrient-dense options are ideal, all calories "count" the same nutritionally regardless of source. Moderating intake to expend more energy than consumed allows avoiding excess weight gain.

Hydration is another integral part of nutrition. Water supports digestion, circulation, detoxification and overall functioning. Adequate intake is around 2 liters for women and 3 liters for men daily from beverages and food. Signs of underhydration like fatigue or headaches signal drinking more is needed.

Understanding how to assemble balanced meals and snacks matters too. Focusing on whole, minimally processed foods like fruits, veggies, beans, grains and nuts ensures nutrition without excess sodium, sugar or additives. Moderation and variety of plant foods are key principles.

Aiming for proper portion sizes provides enough calories while curbing overeating. Visual guides like a fist or palm for grains and dense proteins help gauge reasonable amounts. Serving vegetables in abundance offers more volume for fewer calories. Avoiding distractions helps foster mindful eating within proper portions.

Thinking in terms of balanced plates or bowls offers an intuitive framework for vegan meals. Aim for 1/2 vegetables plus about 1/4 each whole grains and plant proteins like beans or tofu. This template offers fat, fiber, vitamins and minerals in proper balance.

Certain optimal dietary patterns have emerged too. For instance, predominantly or exclusively plant-based Mediterranean approaches with fruits, vegetables, grains and healthy fats like olive oil confer benefits for longevity and disease prevention.

On the flip side, limiting processed meat and sweets in the Western-style diet improves health over the long term by reducing inflammation and risk of related conditions like heart disease and diabetes.

A whole foods plant-based diet centered on unrefined fruits, vegetables, beans, nuts and seeds provides great nutrition without much need for oils added in cooking or processing. Focusing on a rainbow of produce delivers a range of antioxidants and phytonutrients too.

Some familiarity with key nutrients aids meal planning. For example, citrus, peppers, broccoli and strawberries offer much-needed vitamin C. Dark leafy greens, legumes and avocados provide iron. Fortified non-dairy milks can serve as calcium sources. Being aware of major vitamins, minerals and their food sources helps ensure their steady intake.

Reading nutrition labels also helps identify key amounts of protein, fats, sodium, vitamins and minerals provided per serving. This allows comparing products and selecting more optimal choices.

No one eats perfectly all the time, so cultivating balance and moderation over the long term is ideal. Paying attention to how different foods make you look and feel helps determine optimal personal nutrition. Pairing a plant-strong diet with active lifestyle supports lifelong health and energy.

Understanding nutrition basics empowers making wise plant-based food choices. Combining adequate calories with proper hydration, portions and variety ensures you feel and function your absolute best while powering your body with all the essential vitamins, minerals and nutrients it needs to thrive.

Protein and the Plant-Based Diet

Protein is an essential macronutrient that serves many vital functions in the body. It makes up the muscles, organs, hormones, enzymes, immune cells and more. Unlike carbohydrates and fats, the body cannot store protein. Therefore, we must consume protein-containing foods regularly. The good news is that plant-based diets can easily meet all protein needs.

The building blocks of protein are amino acids, which link together in chains to form proteins. Our bodies can produce some amino acids, but nine amino acids must come from food. These nine are called the essential amino acids. Foods that contain all nine essential amino acids are considered complete proteins.

Animal products like meat, fish, eggs and dairy are complete proteins. Plant foods are often incomplete proteins, meaning they lack one or more essential amino acids. By eating a variety of plant protein sources over the course of a day, you can obtain all the essential amino acids your body needs.

Despite the persistent myth that vegetarians and vegans are protein deficient, research shows plant-based diets provide sufficient high-quality protein for optimal health. As long as calorie needs are met and a variety of plant proteins are eaten, protein requirements are typically exceeded on a vegan diet.

Several factors influence how much protein an individual needs. Your age, muscle mass, activity level and health status all play a role. The Recommended Daily Allowance (RDA) for protein is 0.8 grams per kilogram of body weight for average adults. Highly active people need more - about 1.2 to 2.0 grams per kilogram. But deficiencies are uncommon on a reasonably varied plant-based diet.

Many delicious plant foods are rich in protein, including:

- Beans and legumes: chickpeas, lentils, soybeans
- Nuts and nut butters: almonds, walnuts, cashews
- Seeds: hemp, chia, flax, pumpkin
- Whole grains: quinoa, oats, amaranth
- Tofu and tempeh
- Edamame
- Leafy greens
- Nutritional yeast
- Vegan protein powders: soy, pea, rice, hemp

Combining different plant proteins at meals helps provide a complete amino acid profile. Rice and beans is a classic example. Pairing grains with legumes, nuts or seeds maximizes protein quality. Even greens and veggies contain small amounts of protein that contribute.

Plant proteins found in whole foods have extra nutritional benefits compared to isolated animal proteins. Fiber, antioxidants, minerals and phytochemicals all come as part of the package with plant proteins.

Some tips for getting enough protein from plant-based sources:

- Incorporate protein-rich foods like beans, tofu or tempeh at each meal.
- Snack on nuts, seeds, edamame and nut butters.
- Start the day with a protein-packed smoothie or oatmeal.
- Choose higher protein options like quinoa or buckwheat instead of white rice or pasta.
- Enjoy vegan protein bars or shakes when appetite needs a boost.
- Eat a wide variety of plant foods each day for a complete range of amino acids.

The plant-based protein recommendations for athletes, bodybuilders and highly active people are essentially the same. Increased calorie and carbohydrate intake balances the extra protein needs. But a vegan diet has been shown to support intense training and athletic performance.

In summary, it is easy to fulfill all your protein requirements on a plant-based diet. By eating sufficient calories and enjoying a diverse range of protein-rich plant foods, you will obtain the full range of essential amino acids your body requires for optimal health.

Essential Vitamins and Minerals in a Vegan Diet

A balanced vegan diet can easily provide all the vitamins and minerals needed for optimal health. Being aware of key nutrient functions and plant-based sources helps ensure adequate intake.

First, vitamin B12 merits special attention. Needed for nerve and blood cell health, B12 is not reliably found in plant foods. Vegans must rely on fortified foods or supplements for this essential vitamin. Common vegan sources include fortified non-dairy milks, nutritional yeast, cereals and B12 supplements. Consistently getting the recommended 2.4mcg daily prevents deficiency.

Another key focus is vitamin D, which aids calcium absorption for bone health and supports immunity. Sunlight triggers natural vitamin D production, but food sources are still important for those with limited sun exposure. While rare in plants, some options like fortified plant milks and mushrooms contain vitamin D. Safe sun exposure, supplements or fortified foods help vegans obtain 600-800 IU daily.

Vitamin C is also essential, supporting collagen formation, absorption of some nutrients, brain function and immunity. Luckily it is abundant in many fruits and vegetables. Citrus fruits, red peppers, broccoli, strawberries, tomatoes and potatoes offer excellent sources able to provide the 75-90mg needed each day.

Plant foods can also easily deliver other B vitamins like riboflavin, niacin, and folate. These aid metabolism, nerve health and cell growth. Whole grains, nuts, nutritional yeast, avocados, mushrooms and spinach provide excellent quantities of these essential Bs for energy.

Turning to minerals, calcium for strong bones and teeth tops the list. While dairy provides calcium, plant sources like fortified plant milks, kale, broccoli, almonds and tofu supply ample amounts as well. Eating these foods regularly can provide the 1000mg adolescents and adults need daily.

Zinc and iron also deserve attention. Zinc supports immunity and cell growth, while iron enables blood oxygen transport and energy metabolism. Beans, nuts, seeds, tofu, cashews, quinoa and pumpkin seeds offer plant-based zinc sources. For iron, eat lentils, spinach, raisins, swiss chard and fortified cereals. These provide zinc and iron without meat.

Iodine is crucial for thyroid health and metabolism. Though rare in plants, iodized salt and seaweed provide vegan iodine sources. Using iodized salt in cooking regularly helps satisfy the 150mcg needed daily. Nori sheets used in sushi also supply helpful amounts.

Potassium, magnesium and selenium round out key minerals to emphasize. Potassium regulates fluid balance and heart function. Magnesium aids bone health and muscle function. Selenium supports immunity and reproduction. These are amply found in bananas, avocados, spinach, beans, lentils, cashews, oats and brown rice.

With sound meal planning, these vitamins and minerals are all attainable without supplements by eating a varied diet. However, supplements can act as an insurance policy when diet falters. A standard multivitamin or targeted single nutrient supplements help hedge nutritional bases when needed.

Some groups like older adults, pregnant women, strict vegans or those with absorption issues may especially benefit from strategic supplementation. In these cases, discuss options with a healthcare provider. But for many balanced vegans, a well-planned diet should satisfy all vitamin and mineral needs.

Certain lifestyle strategies complement obtaining enough essential vitamins and minerals. Getting regular sun exposure aids vitamin D needs. Soaking beans and grains before cooking boosts mineral absorption. Vitamin C aids iron absorption, so pairing citrus with iron-rich foods maximizes benefits.

Being attentive to vitamin and mineral nutrition from the start prevents pitfalls. Over time, familiarity with plant-based sources of these essentials will become second nature. With knowledge and planning, plant-powered menus can serve up every vital nutrient the body requires for top health and performance without fail.

Balancing Macronutrients for Optimal Health

Macronutrients are the nutrients our bodies need in large amounts. They provide calories, or energy, to power our bodily functions. The three macronutrients are carbohydrates, proteins, and fats. Mastering macronutrient balance promotes health through optimal energy, weight management, and disease prevention.

Carbohydrates include sugars, starches, and fiber found in fruits, vegetables, grains, and legumes. The Dietary Guidelines for Americans recommend getting 45-65% of calories from carbs. Complex carbs like beans and whole grains provide lasting energy.

Protein makes up muscles, organs, hormones, and more. It should represent 10-35% of calorie intake. Protein needs depend on factors like age, activity level, etc. Plant proteins like lentils, nuts, tofu are excellent options on a vegan diet.

Fats help absorb vitamins, insulate the body, and produce hormones. Even though high-fat diets are popular, the recommendation for health is 20-35% of calories from fat. Focus on heart-healthy unsaturated fats like those in avocados, seeds, olive oil.

Each macronutrient serves vital roles, so a balance is ideal. Drastically reducing one will leave you low on energy and key nutrients. The optimal ratio is based on your total caloric needs, activity level, and health goals.

A whole foods plant-based diet naturally supports macronutrient balance. Abundant complex carbs come from vegetables, fruits, whole grains and legumes. Healthy fats are found in nuts, seeds, avocados and plant oils. Plant proteins are derived from beans, lentils, tofu, tempeh and more.

Vegan diets tend to be higher in carbohydrates and lower in fat compared to the standard American diet. This carb-heavy ratio is linked to many health benefits like lower risk of heart disease, diabetes, and obesity. But pay attention to overall eating patterns.

Focus on getting antioxidants, phytonutrients, and fiber from whole food carbs like fruits, veggies, beans, whole grains. Limit heavily processed carbs and added sugars, which spike blood sugar without nutritional payoff.

Increase healthy fats by enjoying nuts, seeds, avocados, and moderate amounts of plant oils. Reduce saturated fat from coconut, palm oil, fried foods, and processed vegan products. Prioritize whole food fats over isolated oils.

Without planning, vegans can fall short on protein compared to other macronutrients. But combining different plant proteins ensures adequate intake. Beans, lentils, tofu, seitan, tempeh, edamame, nuts, seeds and whole grains all contribute.

Here are some tips for optimizing your macros on a plant-based diet:

- Base meals on low-glycemic complex carbs like beans, oats, quinoa
- Load up on non-starchy veggies for micronutrients
- Include healthy plant fats like avocado or tahini
- Don't skimp on plant proteins like tofu, tempeh, beans, lentils
- Snack on nuts and seeds for protein and healthy fats
- Limit processed carbs and sugars
- Track macros with an app if trying to reach certain ratios

- Work with a dietitian to tailor your ideal macronutrient balance

A whole foods plant-based diet with plenty of variety makes balancing macros intuitive and effortless. Pay attention to portions of protein, fat and carbs at meals. Listen to your hunger cues. Stay active to burn calories. Hydration also affects energy and appetite.

Fine-tuning your personal carb/protein/fat ratio to match activity level, health status and goals may provide benefits. But whole plants naturally have ideal proportions. Focus on quality sources and your body will find the balance.

Addressing Nutritional Concerns in Veganism

Transitioning to a vegan diet often raises questions about meeting nutrient needs without animal products. However, with sound information and planning, all key vitamins, minerals and macros can be obtained from plant-based sources alone.

Protein is one top concern. Nearly all plants contain some protein, so contrary to popular belief, deficiency is exceptionally rare on a vegan diet. As long as calorie needs are met and a variety of plants like beans, nuts, grains and veggies are eaten, protein needs will be satisfied. Athletes and bodybuilders alike build muscle on plant proteins. Combining complementary sources like rice and beans maximizes amino acid balance as well. With a small bit of nutrition knowledge, vegans can get sufficient high quality protein.

Another issue often raised is iron, which aids blood oxygen transport and energy production. Iron is abundant in beans, lentils, spinach, pumpkin seeds, cashews and raisins. Pairing iron-rich foods with vitamin C sources like citrus fruits boosts absorption. Unless already deficient, well-planned vegan diets provide ample iron even during growth spurts or menstruation. Those at risk of deficiency can consider supplements as well.

Calcium for bone health is also a concern, but readily available in plant-based forms. Fortified plant milks offer convenient calcium sources. Greens like kale and broccoli also deliver ample calcium. Tofu, sesame seeds and almonds further contribute to daily needs.

Regularly eating these calcium-rich foods supplies the 1000mg required daily. Supplements can also assist those who prefer extra insurance.

Another nutrient, vitamin B12, deserves attention since it is not reliably found in plants. Vegans must rely on fortified foods or supplements for their B12 intake. Common vegan sources include fortified plant milks, nutritional yeast, cereals and B12 supplements. Getting the recommended 2-3mcg daily prevents any deficiency.

Finally, long chain omega-3 fatty acids like EPA and DHA are often assumed to only come from fish. But seaweed, algae and microalgae supplements actually provide vegan-friendly EPA and DHA sources. Walnuts, chia seeds, hemp and flax also contain anti-inflammatory omega-3 ALA. A small supplement or sprinkling these foods into meals offers easy omega-3 intake for vegans.

With sound information, vegans can overcome just about any nutritional concern. But seeking guidance from a healthcare provider, dietician or nutritionist when making major dietary changes is always wise. Bloodwork offers an objective way to monitor nutrition. A balanced whole foods plant-based diet should provide all needed vitamins and minerals. But supplements, fortified foods or strategic meal planning provide extra assurance as needed on an individual basis.

Beyond nutrition, social and psychological hurdles may arise when adopting veganism. Difficulties with family traditions, dining out and dealing with peer pressure present challenges. Building a support system helps normalize the lifestyle. Connecting with other vegans and vegetarians generates camaraderie and advice for navigating social situations.

On an emotional level, some may grieve forsaking familiar animal products. Allowing time to adjust while reminding oneself of the reasons behind veganism helps this pass. Counseling, meditation and self-care practices can also help process feelings and build resiliency.

Being prepared for responses from family and friends is also useful. Kindly informing loved ones about your transition and providing resources helps garner support. Social media groups offer advice for deflecting teasing or peer pressure as well. With compassion and consistency, usually others will accept veganism over time.

Patience and flexibility additionally help smooth out kinks in the journey. Implementation challenges or minor setbacks are normal. Sticking with it gets easier. Progress over perfection is the goal - every vegan-friendly meal makes a meaningful impact. With commitment and community, the benefits outweigh any struggles.

In short, nearly any nutritional or social concern accompanying the transition to veganism can be handled with planning, support and perseverance. The learning curve is surmountable. Drawing on sound nutrition principles, ample resources and self-compassion paves the way for success. Before long, reaping the rewards of plant-based eating becomes second nature.

CHAPTER 3

TRANSITIONING TO A PLANT-BASED DIET

Preparing Your Kitchen

Transitioning to a plant-based diet is easier when you set up your kitchen for success. A well-stocked, vegan-friendly kitchen makes sticking to healthy, plant-powered meals effortless. Follow these tips to get your space ready:

Clean Out and Organize

Start by removing any non-vegan items from the pantry, fridge and freezer to avoid temptation. Donate unopened foods to local charities. Sort through and neatly organize any products you'll still use to maximize accessibility.

Group like items on shelves. Store snacks separately from meal ingredients. Place oils, vinegars and other flavor boosters close to the stove. Keep fruits and veggies visible so they don't get buried. A labeled, organized pantry prevents buying duplicates.

Stock Up On Plants

Fill your kitchen with an array of colorful fruits, vegetables, whole grains, beans, lentils, nuts, seeds and plant-based proteins. Shop the perimeter first when grocery shopping. Let produce guide your meal planning.

Pre-prep veggies for grab-and-go convenience by washing, chopping and storing them in containers. Freeze bananas and berries for smoothies. Soak and cook beans in batches for hassle-free protein. A well-stocked kitchen makes plant-based cooking a breeze.

Get Equipped

Ensure you have the essential tools for simple plant-based cooking. Good knives, cutting boards, pots and pans are kitchen basics. A blender or food processor streamlines prep.

Helpful appliances include an air fryer for oil-free cooking, a high-speed blender for smoothies, a pressure cooker for fast bean dishes, and a spiralizer for veggie noodles. Invest in useful gadgets over time that save you effort.

Season Well

Herbs, spices and salty condiments add flavor to plants and transform same-old ingredients into new dishes. Stock up on salt, pepper, vinegars, mustard, soy sauce, miso paste, nutritional yeast, hot sauce and any favorite seasoning blends.

Keep fresh herbs on hand like basil, thyme, cilantro and parsley. Expand your spice rack with cumin, paprika, turmeric, chili powder and more. Quality ingredients elevate simple meals.

Research Recipes

Explore vegan blogs and cookbooks for inspiration on how to prepare plants in delicious ways. Find recipes for breakfasts, snacks, main and side dishes, desserts, and more. Start a collection of go-to recipes your household enjoys.

Understand how to use plant-based ingredients like tofu, tempeh, seitan, etc. Learn cooking techniques like roasting, steaming, sautéing and baking. Trying new flavors and cuisines makes meal prep fun.

Consider Culinary Goals

Decide any parameters to help guide food choices like budget, nutrition, time constraints, food sensitivities, etc. You may want quick and easy meals, kid-friendly options, low-fat recipes, etc. Define priorities to streamline planning.

Set Your Space Up for Success

A thoughtfully organized, equipped and stocked kitchen makes sticking to plant-based eating effortless. Keep your pantry and fridge filled with an array of delicious whole foods. Surround yourself with seasonings, gadgets and recipes you love. Soon plant-based cooking will feel like second nature.

Plants You Should Start Loving

One of the joys of plant-based eating is discovering and enjoying a wide variety of nourishing foods from the plant kingdom. Certain veggies, fruits, nuts, seeds, herbs and whole grains offer especially impressive nutritional benefits that make them staples for any vegan. Getting to know these plant superfoods helps ensure optimal nourishment.

Leafy greens top the list. Kale, spinach, swiss chard, arugula, romaine and other greens bursts with vitamins, minerals, antioxidants and fiber. Enjoyed fresh in salads, sautéed, or blended into smoothies, these leaves supply a day's worth of nutrients in one hearty portion. Their endless versatility and dense nutrition make greens a cornerstone of healthy vegan diets.

Brightly colored produce like carrots, sweet potatoes, tomatoes, beets, berries and citrus fruits also impart beneficial phytonutrients. These plant pigments reduce inflammation, improve cellular communication, protect against diseases and enhance health in numerous ways. Work to "eat the rainbow" by enjoying a colorful variety of these antioxidant-rich fruits and vegetables.

Cruciferous vegetables - broccoli, cauliflower, kale, cabbage, Brussels sprouts and bok choy - offer unique benefits too. Containing compounds that help balance hormones and detoxify, they defend against chronic diseases. Their anti-cancer effects are well-established. At least 1-2 servings of these nutrient powerhouses daily does a body good.

Beans and legumes including lentils, chickpeas, black beans and peas also deserve ample love. Packed with plant-based protein, fiber, iron, magnesium, potassium and zinc, they nourish the body in myriad ways. Their amazing versatility allows enjoying them in everything from stews to burritos to falafels and beyond. As staples in many cultures' cuisines, they satisfy and nourish.

Nuts and seeds also supply important advantages. Hemp, chia, flax, walnuts and almonds overflow with anti-inflammatory omega-3 fatty acids, protein and essential minerals. Nut and seed butters, milks and yogurts make enjoying their benefits effortless. An ounce a day of a variety protects against disease and provides key nutrients.

Herbs and spices including turmeric, cinnamon, cayenne, garlic, ginger and black pepper liven up dishes while protecting health. Their anti-inflammatory and antioxidant properties defend against chronic conditions and diseases. Explore different herbs' and spices' perks to amplify food's therapeutic effects.

Don't overlook whole grains like oats, quinoa, brown rice, buckwheat and millet either. High in B vitamins, fiber, protein and minerals, they provide steady energy, keep you full and nourish the body from head to toe. Opting for whole grains over refined ones maximizes these benefits.

Mushrooms even offer valuable nutrition. Varieties like maitake, shiitake and reishi contain compounds that boost immunity and activate immune cells. Full of fiber, potassium and vitamin D, they complement plant proteins too. Consider meaty mushrooms health-boosting staples.

Fermented foods also positively influence digestion and immunity. Sauerkraut, kimchi, miso, tempeh and pickles contain beneficial probiotics that support gastrointestinal and overall health. A scoop or two of these foods routinely makes good nutritional sense.

Lastly, don't forget hydrating fruits and vegetables like cucumbers, melons, pineapple and grapefruit which provide fluids. Combining produce, herbs and legumes creates endless flavor and nutrition possibilities. Discovering new-to-you plant offerings keeps eating healthfully exciting.

Making a point to regularly enjoy these nutritional superstars ensures vegan diets maximize benefits. Focus on finding tasty ways to incorporate greens, beans, nuts, seeds, mushrooms, herbs, phytonutrient-rich produce and whole grains in routines for optimal wellness. Let their dietary powers enhance health, vibrancy and longevity.

Gradual Transition vs. Overnight Change

Shifting to a plant-based diet is a big change. Whether you ease into it or go vegan overnight is a personal choice. There are advantages and drawbacks to each approach. Evaluate your motivations, commitment level and circumstances to determine the best path.

Gradual Transition

Phasing in a plant-based diet over weeks or months allows your tastes, habits and cooking skills to adjust at a comfortable pace. A gradual transition may increase long-term sustainability for some individuals.

Start simple by incorporating more meatless meals each week. Swap animal proteins for plant proteins like beans or tofu. Keep favorite omni dishes, but veganize them. This familiarity helps ease the transition.

Expand food exploration to try new produce, grains, spices and cuisines. Let curiosity guide you. Adding plant-based milks, cheeses and meat substitutes also helps during this shift.

As plant-based eating becomes habit, you may naturally begin reducing animal products without effort. Gently challenge yourself to keep progressing. But make changes at your own speed.

Listen to your body's cues. Increase exercise and fiber intake to ease digestion. Add B12 and track nutrition to avoid deficiencies. Don't restrict - focus on adding plants versus omitting foods during this phase.

Join vegan communities for advice and support. Surround yourself with resources to facilitate the journey. Set manageable goals and celebrate small wins. Allow the process time without self-judgment.

Overnight Switch

Some people feel empowered ditching animal products completely overnight. They want a definitive transition point. This abrupt change provides momentum and focus.

Carefully prepare so you have proper mindset, education and tools first. Stock up on plant staples like grains, beans, milks, etc. Explore recipes. Meal prep to remove guesswork and temptation during the adjustment.

Understand nutrition to meet needs on a vegan diet. Plan balanced meals and snacks. Take B12. Consider deficiencies you may be prone to based on past eating habits. SUPPLEMENT if bloodwork shows low iron, etc.

An immediate switch requires grit during the initial period as your habits change. Cravings, social pressures, and logistical challenges will arise. But staying plant-perfect from Day 1 establishes new patterns faster.

Joining a vegan program provides structured guidance. Or create a support system with friends or online communities. Don't hesitate to ask for help in moments of doubt.

After the first few weeks, your tastes adapt, new habits form and motivation solidifies. Continued education and growth are still essential. But you build momentum after pushing through the hardest part.

Assess Your Needs

Reflect on your personality, motivations and lifestyle to determine the best path. Gradual may work well if:

- You want gentle, sustainable change
- Cooking/shopping skills need development

- Your family/social circle eat meat
- You need time to adjust psychologically

Overnight may work well if:
- You crave definitive change
- You're highly motivated
- You're able to meal prep/cook
- You have good social support

There's no right or wrong approach - it's about finding the method you can adhere to long-term. Be honest with yourself. Undertaking this lifestyle change requires commitment as habits reshape.

Listen to your intuition. Remaining open and patient with yourself smooths the journey, gradual or overnight. Celebrate every plant-based meal as progress. Your health and wellbeing will thank you.

Dealing with Cravings

Cravings for familiar animal products can arise when adopting veganism, especially in the beginning. But with the right strategies, plant-based eaters can overcome temporary urges and retrain tastebuds to appreciate satisfying vegan fare. Conquering cravings requires understanding their psychological and biological drivers along with having healthy substitutions handy.

First, reflect on the emotional or social reasons behind cravings. Memories and cultural traditions attached to meat, dairy and eggs may heighten desires initially. Feelings like anxiety, boredom or frustration can also trigger cravings for comfort from familiar foods. Examining and addressing the root causes reduces their power over choices.

Cravings may also stem from falling into routines and not exerting full willpower. Making active decisions and intentionally planning meals counters mindless grazing. Stocking vegan snacks provides healthy convenience options too. Building new rituals around plant-based foods forgoes old food associations over time.

Biologically, temporary withdrawal from compounds like cheese proteins or meat fats during the transition can spark cravings until the body adjusts. Allowing time for tastebuds, metabolism and hormones to adapt to plant foods helps minimize this. Recognizing cravings often pass in 15-20 minutes also encourages riding them out.

When urgent cravings strike, having satisfying plant-based substitutions on hand offers a quick fix. Meat flavors and textures can be mimicked with fortified faux meats. Non-dairy ice creams or yogurts deliver calcium without dairy. Snacks like roasted chickpeas or nuts provide crunchy satisfaction.

Preparing vegan versions of traditionally non-vegan comfort foods helps conquer cravings as well. Lentil sloppy joes, cauliflower buffalo wings and walnut tacos offer craveable flavors without animal products. Explore vegan recipes that put a plant-twist on familiar dishes.

Distraction techniques help override obsessive thoughts of craved foods too. Calling a friend, exercising, absorbing hobbies, playing games or listening to music shifts mental focus away from cravings until they fade. Visualizing health goals further crowds out thoughts of giving in.

If an occasional craving becomes too strong, enjoying a small amount of the desired food may get it out of your system while keeping overall eating aligned with veganism. Beating yourself up over slip-ups undermines the journey - progress trumps perfection.

Looking at cravings as opportunities for self-discovery and growth sparks positive change too. Examining why you really want cheese or ice cream leads to insights about habits, emotions and needs for compassion. Each conquered craving builds grit and integrity.

Orchestrating your spaces by removing non-vegan items and prominently placing fruits, nuts or other go-to foods eliminates tempting cues and prompts smarter snacking when hungry. Making a list of favorite plant-based foods to eat instead inspires healthy choices too.

Finally, treating yourself periodically with delicious new vegan foods celebrates the journey. Seek out that hot new plant-based restaurant or snack item you've been curious to try as a reward for staying resilient. The excitement of discovering new favorites replaces old cravings.

With understanding and preparation, vegan cravings lose their grip over time. Be patient, address root causes, have go-to substitutes available and realize urges will pass. Each wave of cravings conquered with plant foods makes maintaining the lifestyle second nature until desirability for animal products fades completely.

Setting Yourself Up for Success

Transitioning to a plant-based diet is a major lifestyle change. With preparation and commitment, you can set yourself up for long-term success. Follow these essential tips:

Educate Yourself

Learning everything you can about plant-based nutrition and vegan living ensures you start strong. Study protein sources, recommended supplements, satisfying plant-based cooking methods and more.

Read articles, books, studies and guides. Follow social media accounts and podcasts of vegan experts for ongoing education. Understanding the why and how will strengthen your conviction when challenges arise.

Make a Meal Plan

Planning weekly menus erases the "what's for dinner?" struggle. Mix familiar dishes, simple meals and adventurous recipes. Include complete proteins, produce variety and hydrating foods.

Prep components like grains and beans in advance for quick meal assembly. Stock up on grab-and-go items for busy days. Menu planning prevents poor choices when hunger strikes.

Restock Your Kitchen

Remove non-vegan items and fill your fridge and pantry with plant-based staples. Load up on beans, lentils, whole grains, nuts, seeds and a rainbow of produce. Stock flavor boosters like spices, oils and sauces.

Explore substitute options but don't rely solely on processed vegan products. Focus on cheap, versatile whole foods to keep costs down and nutrition high.

Get Support

Embark on this journey alongside a vegan friend or partner if possible. Join online groups to connect with like-minded people for advice and accountability. Consider a plant-based meetup group in your area for potlucks and dining out companions.

Share your commitment with loved ones and ask them to respect your choice, even if they don't fully understand it. Having a support network makes the transition smoother.

Handle Social Eating

Dining with skeptical family or omnivore friends may be uncomfortable at first. Politely decline dishes containing animal products. Offer to bring a vegan side to share.

Suggest plant-based restaurants. Or check the menu in advance and find an accommodation. Stay focused on your goals for health, animals and the planet. Others will come around when they see you thriving.

Supplement Wisely

Certain nutrients like B12, iron, omega-3s, zinc and calcium may need closer attention until you learn to consistently meet needs through plants. Speak with a doctor or dietitian about helpful supplements. Prioritize nutrients of concern.

Fortified plant milks and cereals, nutritional yeast, microalgae oil and vitamins can fill common gaps during the transition period. Get bloodwork done to check levels.

Stay Persistent

This major shift requires patience, self-compassion and dedication as habits form. There will be cravings, frustrations and well-meaning people questioning your choice. But staying plant-perfect gets easier every day.

Remind yourself constantly why you're doing this whenever you feel discouraged. The animals and planet need you. Each plant-based meal makes a difference. You've got this!

With education, planning and support, your plant-based journey will be smooth, rewarding and sustainable. Approach changes with flexibility. Celebrate small wins and milestones. The effort is so worth it for your health and the greater good!

Lane Payne

CHAPTER 4

PLANNING YOUR PLANT-BASED DIET

Understanding Your Caloric Needs

Determining your optimal daily caloric intake is an important step in planning balanced vegan meals that meet energy needs for your lifestyle and goals. Calorie calculations account for age, sex, height, weight, activity level and other factors to provide rough baseline targets. Tracking intake and weight allows fine-tuning numbers, but understanding general estimating formulas offers helpful starting guidelines.

Several calculations exist to estimate calorie needs. A common one is multiplying your weight in pounds by 12-15 calories depending on activity level. More active individuals use the higher end of the range. Another simple gauge is 14-20 calories per pound for women or 15-25 calories per pound for men depending on lifestyle.

The Mifflin St. Jeor equation offers a more thorough calculation:

For men: 10 x weight (kg) + 6.25 x height (cm) - 5 x age (years) + 5 = total daily calorie need

For women: 10 x weight (kg) + 6.25 x height (cm) - 5 x age (years) – 161 = total daily calorie need

These equations consider height along with the usual age, weight and gender factors to hone in closer on calorie requirements. Entering information into an online calculator provides quick results.

Of course, individual needs vary within these estimates based on muscle mass, metabolism and activity patterns. Tracking intake along with changes in weight and energy levels helps fine-tune numbers to find your personal sweet spot.

Adjusting calories depending on activity and weight goals provides further customization. Those looking to lose weight may aim for the lower end of their range, while extra active individuals need more fuel to optimize performance and recovery. Portion control becomes important to avoid overeating.

But for many transitioning to a vegan diet, maintaining current weight while assuring adequate nutrition is the goal. Eating an abundance of nutritious whole plant foods makes it unlikely to overshoot caloric needs. Focusing on a balanced diet usually results in appropriate intake.

However, some find their appetite spikes when transitioning to plant-based eating. Nuts, seeds, avocados, whole grains and other high-calorie vegan staples must be enjoyed in moderation to avoid weight gain. Portion awareness helps keep excesses in check.

Understanding calorie content provides context for making sound choices too. While protein, carbs and fat garner attention, overall calories still need balancing. Some calorically dense foods like oils and nuts confer great nutrition, but limit portions.

When introducing animal product replacements, be mindful some contain just as many calories as original versions. Opting for whole foods over processed vegan convenience items when possible supports healthful habits.

As intake shifts away from calorie dense meat and dairy foods, the volume of food eaten may seem to increase thanks to plant fiber and water content. This helps satisfy hunger on fewer calories. Adopting the vegan versions of your favorite ethnic cuisines opens up enormous possibilities as well.

With an estimate of your caloric needs in hand, the guesswork of meal planning is reduced. Track intake to finetune your target, but overall eating an abundance of varied whole plant foods should achieve appropriate energy intake without much fuss.

The primary goal is not laser focus on numbers, but finding a comfortable equilibrium where your appetite is satisfied and energy needs fulfilled. Dramatic restriction or forcing intake well outside innate signals causes distress.

Tuning in to your body's cues and responding with wholesome vegan nourishment aligned with your estimated caloric requirement allows a peaceful plant-based lifestyle.

Creating a Balanced Plate

A balanced plate features all the flavors, textures, colors and nutrients your body thrives on. With plants, variety is key for ideal nutrition. Follow basic plant-based plate guidelines at each meal:

Fill Half the Plate with Produce

A rainbow of vegetables and fruits should take up the largest portion. Focus on dark leafy greens, broccoli, cauliflower, cabbage, mushrooms, onions, squash, peppers, tomatoes, carrots, berries and more.

Produce provides a powerhouse of vitamins, minerals, antioxidants and phytonutrients to nourish your cells. It also adds bulk and fiber to meals to promote fullness and digestion. Explore new veggies and fruits often for a range of nutrients.

Include a Protein Source

Beans, lentils, tofu, tempeh, edamame and seitan are great options. Or smaller amounts of nuts, seeds and nut butters. Combining plant proteins ensures you get all essential amino acids.

Protein powers you through the day, helps maintain muscle mass, regulates hormones and repairs tissues. It also keeps you feeling satisfied. Add beans or tofu to greens for a balanced salad.

Incorporate Whole Grains or Starchy Veggies

Choose intact whole grains like brown rice, quinoa, oats, millet or barley. You can also eat starchy vegetables like potatoes, sweet potatoes, squash, peas and corn in place of grains.

Whole grains and starchy vegetables provide important B vitamins, minerals and fiber. They give you long-lasting energy from carbohydrates. Pair them with beans or lentils to make the protein complete.

Include Healthy Fats

Nuts, seeds, avocado, olives and plant-based oils like olive oil contain essential fatty acids that protect your heart and brain health. They also help absorb nutrients like vitamin A, D, E and K.

Just a teaspoon or two delivers beneficial fats and adds richness, creaminess and mouthfeel. Drizzle hemp seed oil over grains. Top salads with toasted walnuts. Blend avocado into smoothies.

Finish with Herbs, Spices and Condiments

Fresh or dried herbs, spice blends, vinegars, mustards, hot sauce and any other flavors help make plant foods irresistible. They add nutrition without calories.

Basil, cilantro, thyme, rosemary, turmeric, cumin, ginger, garlic, miso, nutritional yeast, tamari, balsamic, etc. all enhance flavor and nutrition. Sprinkling herbs before serving maximizes aroma and taste.

Listen to Your Body

No need to portion or calorie count if eating intuitively works for you. Eat until satisfied but not stuffed. Pause halfway and check if you're still hungry. Stop when full.

If monitoring portions and calories is preferred, use a calorie tracking app and meal plan. Make adjustments to find ideal calorie intake for your needs. Portion proteins, grains and fats, while emphasizing unlimited non-starchy veggies.

Building a balanced plate is simple with plants. Fill with colorful produce, add savory protein and whole grains, include healthy fats, and top with flavor boosters. Eat slowly and mindfully, enjoying each nourishing bite.

Weekly Meal Planning 101

Taking time to map out weekly vegan meals sets you up for nourishing success. Though planning sounds rigid, it simply entails jotting down ideas for meals, snacks and recipes to guide grocery shopping and prepare plant-based eating. Approaching this thoughtfully without overcomplicating makes sticking to healthy veganism smooth as can be.

Start by brainstorming broad meal ideas that sound appealing for each day's breakfast, lunch and dinner. These may be general like "green smoothie bowl" or "lentil soup" rather than recipes. Listing out staple ingredients needed like plant milk, tofu, veggies etc helps build grocery lists too.

To spur creativity, browse vegan blogs, cookbooks or recipe sites for inspiration. Make notes of any meals that catch your eye to try out that week. Planning 5-6 dinner ideas with leftovers for lunches avoids monotony.

Building the plan around seasonal produce ensures maximum freshness and affordability. What fruits and vegetables are at peak ripeness and value that time of year? Menu planning around seasonal bounty makes shopping easy.

It can be helpful to focus each week's meals around a few key versatile ingredients used in different ways. For example, do a "cauliflower" or "lentil" themed week utilizing them in various recipes as staple elements. This simplifies shopping and cooking.

Don't forget snacks and staple items like breads, non-dairy milk, nut butters, hummus etc. These round out meals and power you through busy days. Having yummy snacks on hand prevents grabbing less healthy convenience options in hunger.

Planning make-ahead items builds in efficiency too. Soups, bean dishes, casseroles and many other plant-based recipes can be prepped in batches for quick meals later. Consider which recipes can be doubled and frozen or refrigerated to save time.

That said, leave some flexibility for nights when schedules are busy or motivation lags. Having frozen veggie burgers, canned soups or easy pasta jars on standby offers fast, foolproof dinners as needed.

After brainstorming general meal ideas, make a detailed shopping list of every ingredient needed for the week ahead. Check staple items and only note what needs restocking to maximize shopping efficiency.

Before shopping, take stock of current pantry and fridge items needing use. Incorporate these into recipes and the meal plan to avoid waste - like near-overripe bananas ready for banana bread.

One tactic some find helpful is "ingredient pooling" - combining ingredients needed for multiple recipes rather than shopping for each one separately to maximize versatility. For instance, if two recipes call for garlic, carrots and onion, purchase enough for both meals at once.

At the store, stick closely to your list without veering off track into impulse purchases. But stay flexible - if an unplanned item is on sale or inspires meal ideas, go with the flow. Adjusting on the fly comes with the territory.

Above all, don't overcomplicate the process. Planning is simply about thinking through the week ahead, gathering inspiration from recipes when needed, and making a detailed grocery list. It does not need to be elaborate.

Upon returning home, allocating a few hours to meal prep makes executing everything effortless. Chop produce, cook grains and beans, assemble breakfasts and lunches for the fridge, etc. This sets you up for success when hunger strikes.

During the week, loosely follow your plan adapting as the need arises. Plans simply provide a helpful framework, not rigid requirements. Recalibrate based on changing needs or inspiration in the moment.

Use any leftovers or unused ingredients creatively later in the week where possible. Wraps, soups, bowls and salads allow repurposing odds and ends before they spoil. Waste nothing!

Finally, save recipes used that became new favorites to integrate into future plans. Keep notes on particular meals that gave energy, satisfied cravings or supported fitness goals. Soon, you will have a customized vegan meal plan playbook.

With just a little forethought and organization, weekly meal planning takes the guesswork and stress out of nourishing yourself and your family deliciously. Give it a try!

The Art of Mindful Eating

Mindful eating means engaging all your senses to fully savor each bite. It also involves listening to internal hunger and fullness cues. Practicing mindfulness around eating can profoundly deepen your plant-based journey.

Many of us eat unconsciously, rushing through meals without appreciation. We multitask, get distracted, or eat for emotional reasons. Mindful eating brings our complete awareness to the experience.

The first step is removing distractions and technology when eating. Set the mood to relax and focus solely on your food and its aromas, textures, flavors and colors.

As you see and touch your meal, notice its visual appeal. Engaging multiple senses primes your digestive system for optimal nutrient absorption and satisfaction.

Take a moment to appreciate the journey your food took - from the earth, farmers, markets and your kitchen to nourish you. Give thanks for all who contributed to your meal. This gratitude fosters connection.

Slow way down and chew each bite thoroughly, putting down utensils between bites. Notice how flavors emerge and change as you chew. Appreciate the mouthfeel.

As you swallow, tune into the sensations of satisfaction. Feel how your stomach and body respond. Pause halfway through the meal to check if you're still hungry.

Eating slower gives your brain 20 minutes to get the signal that you're full. Fast eaters often overconsume calories before feeling full. Savoring every bite prevents this.

Pay close attention to how combinations of flavors, temperatures and textures delight your palette. Does something need added acidity, spice or crunch? Taste fully before seasoning.

When cravings arise, explore them with curiosity before acting. Are you truly physically hungry or is the body seeking pleasure, distraction, or emotional comfort?

Separate actual hunger from habit, impulse or stress-driven eating. Only eat when your body sincerely needs fuel or nourishment. Stop when full - not overstuffed.

Notice how your mood and energy shift as you nourish yourself. Reflect on how each food makes you feel physically and mentally. Learn your optimal foods.

Mindful eating reveals the deeper meanings we assign to food and mealtimes. Be aware of emotions, relationships and nostalgia connected to your food choices.

Stay present throughout your meal, not dwelling on the past or future. The ritual of mindful eating is profoundly relaxing and centering.

Savoring every bite transforms eating from mindless consumption to an intentional act of self-care. Developing awareness around food choices empowers you to feed your body, heart and soul.

Tips for Practicing Mindful Eating:

- Eat without multi-tasking or screens
- Appreciate the aromas, flavors, textures
- Reflect on the source of your food
- Focus fully on the experience of tasting
- Eat slowly, chew thoroughly, pause between bites
- Notice when you feel satisfied or full
- Explore emotional connections to cravings or food choices
- Relax and savor each nourishing component of your meal

Commit to eating one meal per day mindfully. You'll carry over this presence to other meals naturally. Soon, you'll notice when you need nutritious whole foods versus unsatisfying empty calories. Mindful eating nourishes you on all levels - body, mind and spirit.

Tips for Grocery Shopping on a Budget

Adopting a plant-based diet is often cost-effective since staples like beans, rice, and in-season produce tend to cost less than animal products. But sticking to a grocery budget still takes some strategy. With smart shopping and meal planning though, vegan diets are quite wallet-friendly.

The first rule is to shop seasonally whenever possible. Produce like berries or tomatoes cost a fraction of the price when purchased in peak season. Seek out what fruits and veggies are freshly harvested at a given time of year and build meals around those.

Buying from farmer's markets or joining a CSA can also net savings on local in-season fare. You get the added benefits of supporting small farms and reduced environmental impact. Shopping markets at closing time may score deals on perishables too.

Checking circulars and sales allows stocking up on shelf-stable staples when they are discounted. Bulk bins for beans, grains and nuts offer additional savings. And don't overlook ethnic grocers which often have low prices on lentils, spices and specialty ingredients.

To cut back on packaged and processed foods, opt for raw ingredients whenever practical. A potato is far cheaper than boxed scalloped potatoes, for example. Whole foods generally provide more nutrition per dollar spent anyway.

Meal planning is crucial for efficiency too. Map out recipes and shopping lists to avoid buying excess ingredients that go unused and spoil. "Ingredient pooling" also ensures fully utilizing food purchased. Waste boosts food costs.

Cooking at home allows control over nutrition and price. Vegan condiments, bacon, sausages etc can be made from scratch for a fraction of store costs. Get familiar with cheap substitutions like beans for meat.

However, don't forgo the occasional vegan convenience food if it makes the diet more sustainable for you. Budgeting in some of these grocery items and meat alternatives prevents burnout. Just use them sparingly.

Explore different plant protein options beyond pricier packaged mock meats regularly too. Tofu, tempeh, beans, lentils, peas and whole grains expand choices at lower costs. Canned fishless tuna offers an affordable protein boost as well.

For leafy greens, buy pre-washed bags of spinach or lettuce on sale and use promptly. Otherwise purchase heads of lettuce, cabbage etc and wash leaves as needed. The per pound cost is lower. Frozen greens provide economical cooking shortcuts too.

When selecting fruits, opt for in-season or frozen varieties. Canned fruits in juice rather than heavy syrup cut added sugars. Bananas, berries, citrus fruits and melons tend to be budget-friendly fresh options in many regions.

Don't assume organic produce is always mandatory either. If cost-prohibitive, conventional vegetables and thicker-skinned fruits still confer benefits. Simply wash well and remove peel when possible.

Gaining familiarity with lower-cost nutritional powerhouses helps too. Foods like carrots, cabbage, squash, rice, beans, oats and potatoes offer excellent value. Base meals around these nutritious staples.

Becoming skilled at repurposing leftovers into new dishes minimizes waste. Turn leftover rice into fried rice, roast veggies into soups, stale bread into croutons. Creative ingredient recycling saves dollars.

Finally, supplements are optional. Rely on fortified foods like plant milks or breakfast cereals to provide calcium, vitamin D, vitamin B12 and omega-3s instead. Whole foods deliver nutrients more economically.

With resourcefulness in the kitchen and smart shopping habits, plant-based eating can readily fit any budget. Prioritize in-season produce, buy bulk, plan meals, and repurpose leftovers. Eating vegan does not have to break the bank.

Lane Payne

CHAPTER 5

QUICK AND EASY PLANT-BASED BREAKFAST RECIPES

Green Smoothie Magic

Starting your day with a green smoothie is an easy ritual with big benefits. These nutrient powerhouses supply a hefty dose of produce along with protein and healthy fats to keep you energized and satisfied. Adapt basic recipes to your personal tastes and reap the rewards.

A green smoothie template includes:

- Leafy Greens - The foundation. Spinach, kale, swiss chard, lettuces, etc. pack vitamins, minerals and antioxidants. Use a few generous handfuls.

- Fruit - For sweetness and to blend smoothly. Bananas, berries, mangoes, pineapple, etc. Mask any bitter greens. Use 1-2 cups.

- Liquid - Water, plant-based milk or juice. Keeps the blend smooth and hydrating. Use 1-2 cups.

- Protein (optional) - Boost staying power. Tofu, nut butter, hemp hearts, chia or plant protein powder work well. Use 2-4 tablespoons.

- Boosters (optional) - Customize nutrition and flavor. Flaxseed, cocoa powder, vanilla, cinnamon, fresh ginger or herbs liven things up. Use 1-2 teaspoons.

Blend ingredients until smooth and creamy. Taste and adjust sweetness/thickness if desired. Pour into a to-go cup and enjoy!

Here are tasty, nutritious combinations:

- PB & J - Banana, strawberries, peanut butter, spinach, plant milk
- Tropical Twist - Pineapple, mango, coconut water, kale
- Chocolate Peanut Butter - Banana, cacao powder, peanut butter, spinach, plant milk
- Strawberry Banana - Strawberries, banana, vanilla protein powder, romaine, almond milk
- Apple Pie - Apples, cinnamon, almond butter, kale, apple juice
- Rise & Shine - Banana, blueberries, almond butter, spinach, oat milk
- Green Power - Cucumber, parsley, pineapple, kale, lime juice, water
- Mean Green - Kale, parsley, green apple, lemon, ginger, water
- Purple Haze - Blueberries, blackberries, banana, spinach, almond milk
- Tropical Green - Mango, papaya, kale, coconut water

Many commercial blenders like Vitamix or Blendtec work great. Or use a personal sized blender for single servings. Get creative with combinations!

Benefits of Green Smoothies:

- Pack in multiple servings of fruits/veggies
- Provide hydration and nutrition first thing
- Are fast, portable breakfasts or snacks
- Help reduce processed/fried foods in diet
- Aid digestion and gut health
- Boost energy levels and mental clarity
- Can contribute to weight loss

- Are kid-friendly and easily customized

Enjoy green smoothies for breakfast, snacks, desserts or anytime. Keep prepped greens in the freezer to simplify throwing together a blend. Rotate your ingredients to ensure a variety of nutrients. Smoothies make nourishing your body delicious!

High-Protein Vegan Pancakes

Fluffy, protein-packed vegan pancakes make the perfect energizing breakfast. This recipe delivers over 20 grams of plant-based protein per serving courtesy of wholesome ingredients like oat flour, chickpea flour and silken tofu. The addition of ground flaxseeds provides an extra dose of omega-3 fatty acids as well. After whipping up this batter, simply cook the pancakes up on a griddle or skillet. Customizable add-ins let you switch it up with everything from berries to chocolate chips.

For the dry ingredients, you'll need:

- 1 cup oat flour
- 1/2 cup chickpea flour
- 2 tablespoons ground flaxseed
- 2 teaspoons baking powder
- 1 teaspoon cinnamon
- 1/4 teaspoon salt

And for the wet ingredients:

- 1 cup unsweetened plant milk
- 1 12.3 oz package silken tofu, drained
- 2 tablespoons maple syrup
- 1 teaspoon vanilla extract

- Coconut oil for the skillet

Optional add-ins:

- 1/2 cup fresh or frozen berries
- 1/2 cup vegan chocolate chips
- 1/4 cup chopped walnuts
- 1/4 cup shredded coconut

To start, whisk together the dry ingredients (oat flour through salt) in a medium bowl until well combined. The flours, flaxseed and leavening agents will become evenly distributed throughout.

In a high speed blender, puree the wet ingredients - plant milk, tofu, maple syrup and vanilla extract - until completely smooth. You want the mixture to become the consistency of a thick batter.

Pour the wet ingredient blend into the dry ingredients and stir just until combined, being careful not to overmix. Some small lumps are fine. Let the batter sit for 5 minutes so the oat flour can soak and soften.

While the batter rests, heat up a large nonstick skillet or griddle over medium. When hot, coat lightly with coconut oil. Working in batches, spoon 1/4 cup scoops of batter onto the skillet. Cook for 2-3 minutes until puffed and bubbles appear on the tops, then flip and cook an additional 1-2 minutes until lightly browned on both sides.

Add any desired mix-ins like blueberries directly into the batter or sprinkle over the tops of the pancakes right after flipping. Chocolate chips will melt nicely when added early.

Serve the protein-packed vegan pancakes warm right off the griddle, topped with maple syrup, fresh fruit, nut butter, coconut yogurt or other desired toppings! Refrigerate any leftover batter up to 5 days.

The blend of plant-based protein sources creates fluffy, satisfying pancake perfection. Oats offer a boost of fiber too. Let the recipe become a weekend breakfast staple, switching up the add-ins to keep things interesting.

No need for eggs or dairy - this recipe proves vegan pancakes can be just as rich and mouthwatering using pantry staples. Top them with fresh berries, bananas, nuts, or a drizzle of maple syrup for added nutrition and flavor. The possibilities are endless.

Whipping up a tall stack with a side of crispy vegan bacon or breakfast sausage makes for a savory sensation. Or for dessert, try them with ice cream or chocolate sauce instead! No matter how they are served up, these high-protein vegan pancakes make an ideal morning meal to fuel your day with plant-powered goodness.

Overnight Oats Variations

Overnight oats make grab-and-go plant-based breakfasts a breeze. Simply mix oats and liquids the night before, and wake up to a ready-to-eat meal. The oats soak up moisture and soften overnight. Customize with mix-ins for endless possibilities.

To make basic overnight oats:

- In a jar or container, combine 1/2 cup rolled oats with 1/2 cup to 1 cup plant milk or yogurt.
- For thicker oats, use less liquid. For creamier, use more. Stir or shake to integrate.
- Refrigerate 8+ hours overnight. The oats will thicken as they soak.
- In the morning, add toppings and enjoy! Keeps 3-4 days refrigerated.

Flavor ideas:

- Apple Pie - Cinnamon, chopped apples, raisins, maple syrup
- Protein Power - Peanut butter, chia seeds, banana, plant protein powder

- Tropical - Diced mango, pineapple, shredded coconut
- Strawberries & Cream - Sliced strawberries, vanilla plant milk or yogurt
- PB & J - Mixed berry jam, peanut or almond butter
- Mocha - Cocoa powder, espresso powder, chocolate chips
- Chai Spice - Chai tea powder, vanilla, chopped dates
- Carrot Cake - Shredded carrots, raisins, cinnamon, walnuts
- Blueberry Muffin - Fresh or frozen blueberries, lemon zest, almonds
- Pumpkin Pie - Canned pumpkin, pumpkin pie spice, pecan pieces

The flavor combinations are endless! Use your favorite fruits, spices, nut butters, extracts, nuts, seeds, plant-based milk or yogurt, sweeteners if desired, and anything else that sounds appetizing.

To boost nutrition, stir in supplements like:

- Ground flax or chia seeds for omega-3's
- Hemp, pumpkin or sunflower seeds for protein
- Cacao nibs or powder for antioxidants
- Nutritional yeast for B-vitamins
- Wheat germ or bran for extra fiber
- Superfood powders like acai, lucuma, maca, etc.

Make a batch on Sunday night to have easy breakfasts ready when busy mornings hit. Overnight oats are highly customizable to your tastes and nutrition needs.

Benefits:

- Extremely fast and simple to make

- Portable to eat on-the-go
- Endlessly adaptable flavors and textures
- No cooking required
- Allows oats to be easily digested
- Can add protein rich nuts, seeds or powders
- Nutrient-dense way to start your day

Wake up to a satisfying plant-powered breakfast without any morning prep. Overnight oats offer a grab-and-go convenience that makes healthy vegan eating effortless.

Tofu Scramble and Vegan "Eggs"

This protein-packed tofu scramble is a quick, easy and delicious vegan breakfast. When crumbled and cooked, extra firm tofu perfectly mimics the texture of scrambled eggs. Adding turmeric tints it sunny yellow while nutritional yeast lends a savory, almost cheesy flavor.

Served with veggies, avocado and whole grain toast, this easy 20 minute recipe provides a complete and satisfying morning meal. For an even heartier option, prepare these easy homemade vegan "eggs" as well using silken tofu and black salt.

For the tofu scramble you will need:

- 1 block extra firm tofu, pressed to remove moisture
- 1 tablespoon olive oil
- 1/2 onion, diced
- 1 bell pepper, diced
- 2 cloves garlic, minced

- 1 teaspoon turmeric
- 1 tablespoon nutritional yeast
- 1/4 teaspoon each salt and pepper
- Chopped fresh parsley or spinach for garnish

For the vegan "eggs":

- 1 12.3 oz package silken tofu
- 1 teaspoon black salt
- 1 teaspoon nutritional yeast
- 1/2 teaspoon turmeric

Optional seasoning and toppings:

- Black salt, paprika, nutritional yeast (for garnish)
- Salsa, guacamole, vegan cheese (for serving)

Start by pressing the extra firm tofu block to remove excess moisture. Wrap in a clean towel and place something heavy on top for at least 20 minutes, until water is expelled. Discard the liquid.

While the tofu presses, prep veggies. Heat oil in a skillet over medium. Sauté onions and peppers until just soft, about 5 minutes. Add garlic and continue cooking 1 minute more.

Crumble the pressed tofu into the veggie mixture. Add turmeric for color and nutritional yeast for flavor. Toss together and cook until tofu is lightly browned, about 10 minutes. Season with salt and pepper.

For the vegan "eggs," simply blend the silken tofu, black salt, nutritional yeast and turmeric until smooth. Heat in a small saucepan until warmed through.

To serve, portion tofu scramble into bowls. Top with a dollop of the silken tofu "eggs" and garnish with parsley, nutritional yeast, paprika or black salt. Enjoy alongside toast, potatoes, avocado and other desired breakfast sides.

This simple, nutritious breakfast comes together in minutes using pantry staples. The seasoned tofu scramble offers a savory, protein-packed start to the day while the whipped silken tofu replicates eggs. Boost nutrition further with whole grain toast or fresh fruit on the side.

Combining different tofu textures results in an incredibly convincing egg mimic. The black salt is key, as it lends an eggy sulfur flavor. Turmeric provides sunshine vibrancy while nutritional yeast adds richness.

Customize your tofu scramble with any favorite veggies - peppers, greens, tomatoes and onions pack extra nutrition. Mix up the spices too, adding cumin, chili powder or herbs like parsley. Side options are endless: rice, beans, potatoes, avocado - anything is fair game.

This high protein morning meal will leave you feeling satisfied and energized without any cholesterol or animal products. Whether you are vegan or just want more plant-based options, this easy recipe proves you can enjoy "eggs" again.

With pantry staples and simple prep, plant-powered breakfast is a breeze. This combo of seasoned tofu scramble and silken tofu "eggs" provides all the savory satisfaction to start your morning off right.

Power-Packed Breakfast Bowls

Breakfast bowls make starting your day a breeze by combining energizing whole foods in one vessel. Building a bowl is as simple as mixing your favorite base, protein, veggies, toppings and dressing. The options for customization are endless.

Bases provide the foundation. Consider oats, millet, quinoa, buckwheat, brown rice, sweet potatoes, beans, lentils or roasted veggies. Choose a single base or mix a few. Portion to 1/2 to 1 cup cooked grains or beans.

Proteins help keep you full and focused. Add tofu, tempeh, seitan, beans, lentils, nuts, seeds, nut butter or vegan yogurt. Aim for 10-20 grams of protein.

Veggies boost nutrition. Add any raw, roasted or cooked veggies you crave. Spinach, kale, zucchini, mushrooms, tomatoes, peppers, onions and sprouts are great choices.

Healthy fats provide satiety. Stir in avocado, olive oil, hemp seeds, walnuts or tahini. Fats aid the absorption of fat-soluble vitamins and phytonutrients.

Toppings lend flavor, texture and fun. Sprinkle on fresh herbs, nuts, seeds, shredded coconut, raisins, diced fruit, nutritional yeast, spices or microgreens.

Dressings and sauces tie everything together. Drizzle on hummus, salsa, tahini, guacamole, nut butter or vinaigrettes. Citrus juice or oils also add brightness.

Adaptations and Ideas:

- Southwest - Quinoa, black beans, corn, avocado, cilantro, salsa
- Mediterranean - Spinach, chickpeas, tomato, cucumber, olives, red wine vinegar
- Thai Peanut - Rice, tofu, cabbage, carrots, peanuts, cilantro, peanut sauce
- Apple Pie - Oats, apple, cinnamon, walnuts, plant milk, maple syrup
- Taco - Potatoes, lentils, lettuce, tomato, onion, vegan cheese, hot sauce
- Macro Bowl - Tofu, kale, quinoa, butternut squash, hemp seeds, tahini
- Breakfast Hash - Sweet potato, spinach, tempeh, onion, nutritional yeast
- Overnight Oats - Soaked oats, chia seeds, almond milk, berries, almonds
- Savory Oats - Oats, mushrooms, peas, olive oil, parsley, black pepper

- Loaded Oats - Oats, plant milk, banana, cacao nibs, peanut butter
- Buddha Bowl - Millet, edamame, carrots, cabbage, ginger dressing
- Harvest Bowl - Roasted veggies, lentils, tahini, pomegranate, pepitas

The simplicity of bowls makes them perfect for creative plant-based meals any time of day. Play with endless combinations of whole foods to hit all your nutrition needs in one satisfying package.

Lane Payne

CHAPTER 6

SATISFYING PLANT-BASED LUNCHES

Buddha Bowl Basics

Buddha bowls have become a staple weeknight dinner thanks to their endless versatility and nutrition. Typically featuring greens, veggies, plant proteins and whole grains, these plant-powered bowls provide balanced convenience.

At its core, a Buddha bowl simply combines grains, protein, produce and healthy fats in an entree-style bowl. Anything goes - tailor them to your taste. Bowls provide a perfect way to clean out your crisper drawer and use up leftover bits creatively.

Start with a base of leafy greens like spinach, kale or lettuce for filler. Then pile on raw, roasted or sautéed vegetables. Good veggie add-ins include broccoli, cauliflower, peppers, onions, mushrooms, carrots, cabbage, sweet potatoes etc.

Top with a protein source. Tofu, beans, lentils, tempeh, edamame, nuts or seeds all add staying power. You could also use mock meats or hearty roasted veggies like eggplant.

Next add a whole grain like quinoa, brown rice, farro or millet. Whole grain noodles, pulses like chickpeas, or starchy vegetables work too. This provides fiber and carbohydrates.

Finish with healthy fats for flavor, satiety and nutrition. Avocado, nuts, seeds, olives, coconut and dressing offer options. Condiments like salsa, hot sauce or hummus also liven up bowls.

When assembling the components, aim for equal portions veggies and protein, a smaller amount of whole grains, and minimal added fats. But customize based on your appetite.

One easy formula is:

- 2 cups mixed salad greens
- 1 cup each two different roasted or raw veggies
- 1/2 to 1 cup beans, lentils or tofu
- 1/2 cup whole grain like quinoa or brown rice
- 1/4 avocado, sliced
- Toppings like salsa, dressing, seeds

Or simplify with a protein, vegetable and grain. Play with different combinations and explorer new ingredients weekly.

Roasting veggies ahead of time streamlines meal assembly. Double roasted veggies and grains when cooking to use throughout the week. Having pre-prepped ingredients ready to mix and match makes Buddha bowls a cinch.

When short on time, use quicker cooking whole grains like bulgur or quinoa instead of brown rice. Canned beans and precooked lentils also save prep. Rely on pantry items like canned corn, tomatoes and olives to quickly round out bowls.

Whirling up a fast salad dressing, tahini or peanut sauce adds big flavor. Easy options include lemon juice, vinegar, salsa, hummus, or store-bought dressing.

Incorporate different ethnic themes into bowls too. Mexican style with quinoa, black beans, salsa and guacamole. Thai with tofu, cabbage, edamame, carrots and peanut sauce. Italian with pesto quinoa, white beans and roasted broccoli.

The possibilities are endless! Buddha bowls make a great weekly meal prep item too - assemble individual portions in containers for grab-and-go lunches or dinners all week.

Creative ingredient swaps prevent boredom. Try new grains like farro or pot barley. Change up your leafy greens - arugula, romaine, kale and spinach all work. Explore new plant proteins, veggies and seasonings weekly.

Buddha bowls provide convenience without sacrificing nutrition or taste. They satisfy cravings with endless flavor and texture options. Best of all, utilizing leftovers prevents food waste for an earth-friendly meal. Bowls lend themselves to creative plant-based cooking at its easiest!

Vegan Sandwiches and Wraps

Sandwiches and wraps make fast, portable plant-based meals and snacks. With whole food ingredients and creative combinations, they can be nutritious as well as delicious. Explore diverse breads, spreads, fillings and components to pack a flavor and nutrition punch.

Breads and Wraps

Choose whole grain or sprouted breads to up the nutrition. Look for fun additions like seeds, nuts or herbs baked in. Plant-based wraps offer variety, as do lettuce or collard green leaves.

Spreads and Condiments

Spreads add moisture and bring flavors together. Hummus, oil-free nut and seed butters, mashed avocado, nut-based cream cheeses and pestos all work great. Mustard, oil and vinegars, hot sauce, relish and tapenades also enliven sandwiches.

Protein Fillings

Packed with staying power, proteins include sliced deli meats like Tofurky or Lightlife, grilled tofu or tempeh, crispy fried chickpeas, roasted eggplant or mushrooms, marinated artichokes, baked or mashed beans, and more.

Veggies and Fruits

Load up sandwiches with raw or cooked veggies for nutrition, texture and brightness. Favorites are lettuce, tomato, cucumber, roasted red peppers, grilled eggplant, sautéed mushrooms, onions, sprouts, shredded carrots, pickled vegetables and sliced fruit like apple or pear.

Crunchy Toppings

For satisfying crunch, add avocado, sprouts, cucumber, roasted veggies, sauerkraut, nuts, roasted chickpeas or tortilla chips. Pump up nutrition with seeds like sunflower, pumpkin, hemp or chopped nuts.

Cheeses and Sauces

Plant-based cheeses, yogurt, nut-based sauces like vegan pesto or ranch, and flavorful hummus or bean spreads make sandwiches creamy and indulgent. A drizzle of balsamic glaze also adds intrigue.

Putting it all Together:

- The Classic - Hummus, cucumber, tomato, spinach, sprouts on whole grain
- Chipotle Black Bean - Smashed black beans, roasted red peppers, avocado, lettuce, chipotle hummus on whole wheat
- Caprese - Marinated artichokes, tomato, basil, vegan mozzarella, balsamic glaze in a wrap
- Tempeh Reuben - Smoked tempeh, sauerkraut, vegan thousand island, swiss cheese on rye
- BBQ Jackfruit - Shredded BBQ jackfruit, coleslaw, avocado, onion in a whole grain wrap
- Mediterranean - Smashed chickpeas, roasted eggplant, tahini sauce, pickled red onions, arugula on focaccia
- Nutty Apple - Almond butter, sliced green apple, spinach, sprouts on whole grain bread

- BLT - Smoky coconut bacon, lettuce, tomato, avocado, vegan mayo on sourdough

The combinations are endless! Use whole food plant-ingredients tailored to your tastes for nutritious sandwiches and wraps.

Plant-Based Pasta Dishes

Pasta makes a delicious, comforting meal for vegans when topped with a variety of plant-based proteins and produce. Explore fun pasta shapes beyond just spaghetti and pair with nutrient-dense sauces for a satisfying dish.

Types of Pasta

For an interesting twist, try pasta shapes like penne, rotini, farfalle, orecchiette, cavatappi, orzo, angel hair, lasagna noodles or ravioli. Choose whole grain or vegetable-blended varieties. Zucchini, beet, tomato or carrot pastas add color and nutrients.

Plant-Based Proteins

Proteins provide staying power. Try sautéed tempeh, Italian veggie meatballs or sausage, marinated tofu, white beans, edamame, lentils, chickpeas, peas or nuts like pine nuts or walnuts. Use 10-15g protein per serving.

Build Flavorful Sauces

Make your own oil-free marinara with crushed tomatoes, garlic, basil and seasonings. Other tasty sauces include almond-based pestos, white bean "alfredo", tahini sauce, sun-dried tomato sauce, vegan "cheese" sauces, olive tapenades and nut-based herb sauces.

Mix in Vegetables

For nutrition and texture, add fresh or roasted veggies like broccoli, spinach, tomatoes, roasted red peppers, mushrooms, carrots, kale, zucchini, eggplant and arugula. Chop or spiralize for fun shapes.

Garnishes and Toppings

Finish pasta with chopped herbs like parsley, basil, oregano or marjoram. Grated vegan parmesan adds flair. Sprinkle on toasted nuts or seeds for crunch. Drizzle with extra virgin olive oil. Freshly ground pepper ties it all together.

Putting it Together:

- Primavera - Spiralized zucchini and carrots, broccoli, peas, sun-dried tomato sauce, pine nuts
- Pesto Pasta - Basil pesto, roasted tomatoes, chickpeas, topped with roasted Brussels sprouts
- Creamy Tomato - Orecchiette, creamy tomato sauce, sautéed tempeh, roasted eggplant, basil
- Cacio e Pepe - Spaghetti, creamy "cheese" sauce, peas, sunflower and pumpkin seeds, black pepper
- Marinara - Rigatoni, chunky marinara, tofu meatballs, roasted red peppers, toasted walnuts
- Spicy Peanut Noodles - Rice noodles, spicy peanut sauce, edamame, broccoli, red pepper flakes
- Pumpkin Alfredo - Farfalle, roasted kabocha squash alfredo sauce, spinach, pine nuts
- Pomodoro - Penne, basil and tomato sauce, white beans, zucchini ribbons, crushed red pepper
- Creamy Mushroom - Rotini, cashew cream sauce, sautéed mushrooms, fresh parsley and dill
- Lasagna - Layered lasagna noodles, tofu ricotta, lentil bolognese, roasted garlic marinara

The pasta possibilities are endless! Use healthy plant-based ingredients tailored to your tastes for nutritious and comforting pasta meals.

Hearty Vegan Salads

Salads offer an easy way to pile on the fresh fruits, veggies, beans, grains and nuts in a vegan diet. But they don't have to be boring or leave you hungry. Building hearty main dish salads with plant-based proteins, healthy fats and toasted nuts or seeds ensures satisfying staying power.

The key is loading up on good vegetarian protein sources. Tofu, edamame, beans, lentils, tempeh and chickpeas all offer options. Roasted veggie slices or cubes like potatoes, beets or eggplant work too. Seitan, soy curls and plant-based meat alternatives provide additional choices.

Beyond greens, fold in nutrient-dense produce like tomatoes, carrots, peppers, broccoli, cauliflower, cabbage, onions, mushrooms, etc. The more colors and varieties, the better. Roasting veggies intensifies flavor.

Boosting texture with nuts, seeds, roasted chickpeas and crunchy elements prevents a mushy salad. Toasted walnuts, pepitas, sunflower seeds, slivered almonds all add interest.

Whole grains take the salad from side dish to main event. Quinoa, wheat berries, rice, pearl barley, farro, and power blends bulk up a salad into a hearty meal. Or substitute starchy veggies like sweet potato.

Healthy fats lend richness, creaminess and mouthfeel. Avocado, tahini or tofu based dressings, infused olive or coconut oils, nuts and seeds all fit the bill. But watch portions, as fats add up quickly.

Incorporate multiple plant-based protein and produce sources to cover all your nutrient needs. For example:

- Chickpeas, lentils, edamame atop spinach with vinaigrette
- Tofu, cabbage, carrots, peppers, cashews and miso dressing
- Beans, quinoa, kale, tomato, avocado with salsa
- Seitan strips, farro, Brussels sprouts, dried cranberries, pecans
- Roasted eggplant, beets, tempeh over lettuce with tahini drizzle
- Edamame, brown rice, carrots, peppers, almonds, ginger dressing

Lightly roasting tougher veggies like cauliflower or broccoli makes them tender but still crunchy. Toast nuts and hardier grains like farro too for extra texture.

Acidic components like lemon juice, vinegars, salsa and hot sauce brighten up salad flavors. Hummus, tahini, nut butters or vegan pesto make creamy dressings.

Keep prepped salad toppings like roasted chickpeas, plant-based bacon bits, croutons or toasted seeds on hand for quick protein boosts. Make enough dressing for several salads at once.

Let the seasons guide your veggie choices too. In summer enjoy corn, tomatoes and zucchini. Fall and winter offer roasted beets, Brussels sprouts, sweet potatoes and kale.

Salads satisfy cravings for comfort foods too. Toss in vegan bacon, creamy dressings and croutons for crunch. Add plant-based cheese or creamy cashew dressing for rich indulgence.

With hearty proteins, tons of produce and satisfying textures and flavors, main dish salads make for nutritious and filling comfort food. They provide a perfect way to load up on high fiber, vitamin-rich greens and vegetables. Dive into salad crafting and discover infinite fresh possibilities!

Quick and Easy Soups

Soups make for comforting, nourishing meals on a plant-based diet. With a simple template, it's easy to whip up flavorful, nutritious soups using vegetables, plant-based proteins, herbs and spices. Keep a batch in the fridge for healthy grab-and-go lunches and dinners.

Start with an Aromatic Base

Sauté onion, garlic, ginger or lemongrass to build a flavor foundation. Cook for 2-3 minutes until softened and fragrant. You can also char vegetables like eggplant or peppers for more depth.

Add Liquid

Broth, coconut milk, nut milks, or water work as the soup base. For creaminess, puree beans, potatoes or soaked cashews into the broth. Use about 4 cups liquid total for a main dish soup. Reduce for a side.

Include Protein-Rich Ingredients

Beans, lentils, quinoa, tofu, tempeh, edamame and peas amp up nutrition. White beans, chickpeas and lentils add heartiness. Tofu cubes provide an easy protein boost. Use 1 to 2 cups cooked protein.

Incorporate Vegetables

Harvest produce straight from the fridge or freezer to use up leftovers. Favorites are carrots, kale, spinach, green beans, zucchini, broccoli, cauliflower, mushrooms, tomatoes and peppers. Chop or blend to your preferred texture.

Season to Taste

Flavor with herbs like cilantro, parsley, basil, oregano, rosemary, thyme and sage. Spices like cumin, paprika, curry powder, coriander, turmeric, cinnamon and chili powder also enliven soups. Add Bragg's, soy sauce, miso or nutritional yeast for savoriness. Fresh lemon or lime juice adds brightness right before serving.

Toppings and Garnishes

Finish soups with fresh herbs, toasteds nuts or seeds, roasted chickpeas for crunch, coconut flakes, hot sauce, croutons, or a swirl of coconut or almond yogurt. A sprinkle of microgreens adds color.

Satisfying Combinations:

- Tomato Basil - Diced tomatoes, basil, white beans, pasta
- Lentil and Squash - Red lentils, butternut squash, cumin, cilantro
- Ramen Zoodle - Zucchini noodles, miso, tofu, mushrooms, spinach
- Thai Coconut - Red curry paste, coconut milk, vegetables, basil
- Tortilla - Black beans, corn, peppers, lime, tortilla strips
- Potato Leek - Potatoes, leeks, almond milk, rosemary
- Broccoli Cheese - Broccoli, onion, nut milk, nutritional yeast
- Minestrone - Kidney beans, veggies, pasta, parsley, Parmesan
- Chickpea and Kale - Chickpeas, kale, veggie broth, garlic
- Split Pea - Split peas, celery, carrots, thyme, smoky seasoning

The simple soup formula allows for endless nutritious combinations using whatever you have on hand. Adjust consistency and flavor to your taste. Soups store well and make healthy, comforting meals.

CHAPTER 7

DELICIOUS PLANT-BASED DINNERS

Vegan Pizza and Flatbreads

Pizza makes for an easy crowd-pleasing meal, and contrary to popular belief, it can be just as delicious when made vegan. Homemade vegan pizza dough lets you control ingredients, or store-bought bases like flatbreads or veggie crusts offer convenience. Pile on your favorite toppings, swap in plant-based cheese, and vegan pizza night can happen any night of the week.

For homemade dough, simply mix flour, yeast, water, salt and a touch of olive oil. Let it rise before stretching or rolling out on a baking sheet or round pizza pan. Whole wheat or white flour both work well.

Pre-made pizza crusts, naan, pitas and flatbreads offer quicker starting points too. Try infused varieties like pesto or sun-dried tomato and herb pizza crust for extra flavor. Cauliflower or butternut squash crusts add veggie nutrition.

Go classic with tomato sauce or get creative with hummus, nut cheese sauces, tahini, pesto or barbecue sauce as the base. Spread thinly to avoid a soggy crust.

Loading up on veggies boosts nutrients while adding texture and flavor. Mushrooms, bell peppers, onions, spinach, zucchini and pineapple all taste great on pizza. Olives, artichokes and tomatoes add interest too.

For protein, tofu cubes, sliced seitan, tempeh bacon and roasted eggplant or chickpeas make delicious additions. They add hearty satisfaction without the cholesterol of meat toppings.

In place of dairy cheese, sprinkle on shredded vegan mozzarella or cheddar for meltiness. Grated nut-based cheeses work too. Or drizzle on flavorful cashew cream cheese.

Finish with fresh herbs like basil or oregano, red pepper flakes for a kick, toasted nuts like pine nuts or walnuts for crunch, or nutritional yeast for a savory, cheesy flavor.

Some enticing vegan pizza topping combinations include:

- Pesto, artichokes, sun-dried tomatoes, spinach, onion
- Barbecue jackfruit, red onion, cilantro
- Cashew cream, caramelized onion, roasted mushrooms
- Tomato sauce, vegan pepperoni, bell peppers, olives
- Hummus, roasted eggplant, zucchini, pine nuts
- Marinara, vegan sausage, red onion, roasted red peppers

Make use of in-season produce like summer squash or fresh basil when available. Change up herbs, spices, sauces and proteins to keep variety high.

Baked potato slices make an unexpected but tasty gluten-free crust option. Corn tortillas also work in a pinch - just pile toppings on and broil until melted.

Let kids get involved in pizza making too choosing fun add-ins like pineapple, vegan cheese and veggie pepperoni for a colorful pie they will love.

To save cost, utilize leftover veggies or bits of precooked grains in the fridge on pizza throughout the week. Flatbreads provide a fast starting point for impromptu pizza anytime.

Vegan pizza offers endless possibilities for creative, healthy and fun plant-based cooking. With the right dough, sauce and toppings, you can enjoy crave-worthy pizza night after night.

Plant-Powered Stir Frys

Stir frying is a quick and healthy cooking method that's perfect for busy vegan lifestyles. Cut veggies and proteins into bite-sized pieces, add sauce ingredients, and stir over high heat for delicious, fast one-pan meals.

Choose a Plant-Based Protein

Tofu, tempeh, seitan and edamame add hearty protein. Chop into cubes for fast, even cooking. Lentils, chickpeas and beans work too. Use 1 to 2 cups protein.

Pick Crisp, Fresh Vegetables

Favorites are broccoli, carrots, bell peppers, onions, green beans, snap peas, mushrooms, cabbage, spinach and asparagus. Mix colors for visual appeal. Cut into small uniform pieces for quick cooking.

Include Aromatics

Garlic, ginger, green onions, lemongrass or shallots provide big flavor for little effort. Sauté briefly in oil before adding other ingredients. Chili paste, curry pastes or miso also add concentrated taste.

Pick a Sauce for Flavor

Stir fry sauces quickly coat ingredients. Use teriyaki, hoisin, sweet chili or stir fry sauces. Nut butters like almond or peanut add creaminess. Liquid aminos, soy sauce, rice vinegar, sesame oil and lime juice also flavor.

Cook in Batches

Avoid overcrowding the pan. Cook proteins separately from veggies for best results. Use a wok or large skillet on high heat. Keep ingredients moving constantly. Work in batches if needed for even cooking.

Serve Over Grains or Noodles

Rice, soba noodles, quinoa or simple steamed veggies round out the meal. Caution with highly starchy noodles as they clump. Cook noodles lightly until just shy of done before stir frying.

Garnish and Finish

A sprinkle of chopped scallions, cilantro, basil or mint adds freshness. Toasted sesame seeds provide crunch. A squeeze of lime and serve! Cleanup is easy with just one pan.

Suggested Combinations:

- Tofu with broccoli and peanut sauce over rice
- Tempeh with snap peas and teriyaki sauce
- Chickpeas with peppers and massaged kale
- Seitan with carrots and orange ginger sauce
- Edamame with cabbage and lime chili sauce
- Lentils with mushrooms and hoisin sauce
- Mixed veggies in a spicy satay sauce

Stir frying makes it simple to whip up balanced vegan meals for dinner in under 30 minutes. Change up flavors and ingredients for endless variety.

Comforting Vegan Casseroles

Casseroles provide the ultimate warm, comforting convenience food. But classic versions tend to rely heavily on meat, eggs and dairy. With a few easy plant-based ingredient swaps though, you can still enjoy all that casserole goodness on a vegan diet.

At their core, casseroles include a protein, vegetables and cream element to hold everything together. Replacing animal proteins with beans, lentils, tofu or soy curls maintains satisfaction. Broccoli, kale, mushrooms, squash, onions, peas and carrots all work well too.

For the creamy base, blended tofu, cashew cream and roasted vegetables pureed into sauces mimic the texture of cheese and cream. Nutritional yeast also adds savory richness. Adding some kind of starch like pasta or rice helps bind it all together.

With these basic elements, you can riff on standard casserole fare. For example, green bean casserole can get a vegan upgrade simply by using mushroom broth or cashew cream as the sauce base instead of cream of mushroom soup. Top with fried shallots instead of onions for crunch.

Tater tot or potato-based casseroles still offer comfort without relying on bacon or beef for flavor. Simply season diced potatoes with spices like onion powder, paprika, parsley and plenty of black pepper before assembling the casserole. Lentils make a perfect high protein substitute for ground beef too.

Broccoli and rice casseroles also convert very easily to vegan recipes. Cooked brown rice or quinoa combined with broccoli, shredded tofu, mushrooms and cashew cream or a blended sauce gets layered or stirred together seamlessly for a creamy bake.

Italinan-style eggplant or zucchini parmesan bakes well using your favorite marinara sauce, sliced veggies, and vegan cheese or a tofu ricotta. For bonus protein, incorporate lentils or beans. Served over pasta, these veggie bakes provide comfort.

Don't forget about mac and cheese - many vegan recipes use blended vegetables, potatoes or cashews to create ultra creamy dairy-free cheese sauces. Combining nutritional yeast and spices amps up the cheesy flavor. Stir with pasta and bake for easy comfort food.

Shepherd's pie also gets an easy makeover. Lentils, veggies and mushrooms simmered in a savory gravy and topped with fluffy mashed potatoes provides an iconic, cozy meal.

With a little creativity, enchiladas, lasagna, pot pies and other classic baked dishes all convert to plant-based comfort. Use whole grain tortillas or noodles, load up on veggies, and utilize seasoned savory sauces for flavor. Hearty add-ins like lentils provide substance too.

Casseroles tend to have long baking times, so take the opportunity to prep filling salads like kale caesar or quick roasted vegetables to enjoy on the side. A refreshing contrast complements the heavy, comforting casserole nicely.

Serving these vegan spins on classic casseroles cuts cravings for old animal-based favorites. They provide the same satisfaction and nostalgia, proving you need not sacrifice comfort or convenience on a compassionate diet. Everything you love about casseroles can be re-created better than ever using plants.

Vegan Burger Variations

Burgers make for hearty, satisfying meals in vegan form with a plant-based patty. Explore creative combinations of beans, grains, mushrooms and more for the protein base. Top with veggies, sauces and buns for crave-worthy plant-powered burgers.

Base Protein Options

- Black bean patties - versatile and popular
- Mixed vegetable and grain patties - add quinoa, millet, etc.
- Lentil or chickpea patties - high protein
- Beet patties - for color and nutrition
- Portobello caps - sturdy and meaty
- Soy protein or veggie burger patties - store-bought for convenience
- Smashed white bean or chickpea patties - for Mediterranean flair

- Walnut-mushroom patties - earthy and nutrient-dense
- Quinoa and brown rice patties - gluten-free
- Tempeh patties - nutty flavor

Mix-In Ideas

- Finely chopped veggies - onion, mushrooms, carrots, zucchini
- Oats or breadcrumbs - to bind
- Nuts or seeds - for crunch and healthy fats
- Herbs and spices - cumin, paprika, parsley, basil, oregano
- Sauces and seasonings - soy sauce, BBQ, Cajun seasoning, etc.
- Condiments - ketchup, mustard, relish, hot sauce, etc.

Toppings and Buns

- Lettuce, tomato, pickles, onion - classic fresh veggies
- Avocado, roasted red pepper, sautéed mushrooms - extra flavor
- Hummus, tahini sauce, chimichurri - creamy spreads
- Cheese, bacon, egg - veganized versions
- Beet bun, whole wheat bun, lettuce wrap - alternate buns
- Sweet potato bun, English muffin, bagel - for variation

Putting it Together:

- Southwestern - Black bean patty, guacamole, lettuce, tomato, spicy vegan mayo on whole wheat bun
- Breakfast - Chickpea patty, vegan cheese, egg, tomato, spinach on English muffin

- Barbecue Lentil - Smoky lentil patty, barbecue sauce, onion rings on sweet potato bun

- Greek - White bean smash patty, hummus, tomato, cucumber, red onion, lettuce on pita

- Beet and Bean - Beet-chickpea patty, cashew cream cheese, arugula on beet bun

- Portobello Caprese - Grilled portobello, melted mozzarella, tomato, basil, balsamic reduction on ciabatta

- Cajun Quinoa - Quinoa-rice patty, sweet potato fries, spicy vegan mayo on pretzel bun

The patty possibilities are endless. Follow formulas or get creative with ingredients. Build burgers to satisfy any craving on a plant-based diet.

One-Pot Wonders

One-pot meals offer the ultimate weekday convenience. With everything cooked together in one vessel, these no-fuss plant-based dinners minimize cooking and cleaning time.

The most familiar one-pot approach is likely stir frying. Simply chop veggies and your protein of choice, then cook everything together quickly over high heat. A sauce ties it all together - choices like teriyaki, peanut, sweet chili and garlic ginger each lend bold flavor. Serve over rice or noodles.

One-pot pasta dishes like vegan bolognese or primavera also come together easily. Cook noodles right in the sauce so everything finishes at once. Just combine marinara or a dairy-free alfredo with your preferred veggies, beans or mock meats.

Chilis, stews and curries work one-pot wonders in the slow cooker, Instant Pot or on the stovetop. Load them up with beans, lentils, veggies and seasonings, and simmer until thick and saucy. They improve over days, so make extra. Serve with rice, avocado, cilantro, etc.

Soups follow a similar convenient path - simply pile chopped veggies, legumes, grains and seasonings into a pot with broth. Minestrone, chili and lentil soups offer flexible options. Simmer until vegetables are tender before enjoying.

For skillet meals, think stir fries without the sauce. Black bean quinoa bowls, tofu veggie bowls and southwest hash come together fast right in the pan. Add extras like avocado, nuts or hot sauce.

Sheet pan dinners maximize ease too. Roast your protein and vegetables together on one sheet until crisp-tender. Try potatoes, broccoli, tofu, chickpeas, cauliflower or other favorites.

Certain electric appliances like Instant Pots take one-pot cooking next level. From beans to stews to porridge, an Instant Pot lets you walk away while food cooks. It infuses convenience into plant-based eating.

When assembling one-pot meals:

- Include your protein - beans, tofu, tempeh
- Feature 2-3 veggies for nutrition
- Add starch if desired - potatoes, rice, quinoa
- Season generously with herbs and spices
- Finish with extras like avocado or nuts

Cooking in batches and reusing leftovers from one-pot mealssaves more time. Lentil soup, roasted veggies and whole grains make great meal starters all week long.

Focus on using seasonal produce so peak ripeness and affordability sync up - carrots, squash and greens in the fall, berries and stone fruits in summer for example.

Cooking just requires a little forethought. Prepping ingredients ahead of time allows throwing together weeknight one-pot meals in under 30 minutes. With one vessel, clean up stays minimal too. Utilize these tips and see how easily delicious plant-based dinners come together.

CHAPTER 8

SNACKS AND DESSERTS

Healthy Vegan Snacks for On the Go

When an energy slump hits or hunger strikes between meals, having satisfying plant-based snacks on hand prevents you from grabbing quick processed fixes. With a little prep, you can stock up on portable snacks to power you through any busy day.

Baked or Raw Energy Bites

Bind together oats, nut butter, seeds, dried fruit, cocoa powder or protein powder and roll into bite-size balls. Bake to set or enjoy raw for extra nutrients. Pack in reusable containers. Flavors like peanut butter chocolate chip, lemon coconut or cherry almond satisfy sweet cravings.

Trail Mix Combinations

Mix together roasted nuts and seeds with dried fruit in single-serve portions. Sweet and salty nuts like almonds, cashews, pecans and peanuts pair well with raisins, cranberries, apricots, banana chips or dates. Add dark chocolate chips or coconut flakes for more interest. Customize to your tastes.

Fresh Fruit and Veggies

Wash and chop produce like carrots, bell peppers, cucumbers, celery, melon cubes, berries or cherry tomatoes. Portion into small containers for healthy convenience. Bring quick-dipping sauces like hummus or nut butter. Swap in roasted chickpeas, edamame or tempeh for more protein.

Smoothies and Protein Shakes

Blend up a smoothie with frozen fruit, greens, nut butters or plant-based milk and protein powder for an energizing drink on the go. Or just make extra in the morning to grab from the fridge later.

DIY Trail Mix Bars

Make chewy granola bars by mixing oats, nut butter, seeds, dried fruit, spices and sweetener if desired. Press into bars, slices or balls and wrap individually. Swap in puffed grains like rice, quinoa or millet for lighter texture.

Popcorn Variations

Toss popcorn with spices like curry powder, chili powder, za'atar or nutritional yeast for flavor. Drizzle with melted nut butter. Sprinkle hemp or pumpkin seeds on top. Portion into bags. Savory popcorn fills you up.

Homemade Energy Gels

Blend dates, nut butter and cocoa powder into a paste. Roll tablespoon scoops into balls and coat in ground nuts, seeds or shredded coconut. Wrap individually for natural fuel on long runs or rides.

Overnight Chia Pudding

Stir chia seeds into plant milk or coconut yogurt in Mason jars. Refrigerate overnight to thicken. Top with fruit, nuts and granola for a grab-and-go breakfast or snack.

Roasted Chickpeas or Edamame

Toss chickpeas or shelled edamame with oil and favorite spices. Roast until crispy. The savory protein satisfies in small portions and keeps well.

Having healthy and satisfying snacks prepared beats vending machine candy bars or chips when hunger hits. With whole food ingredients and creative combinations, you can stay nourished on the go.

Energy Balls and Bars

Portable energy balls and bars make great vegan snacks for an on-the-go boost. Packed with oats, nuts, seeds, dried fruit, coconut and nut butter, these no-bake treats provide lasting fuel. Their sweetness satisfies cravings while ingredients like dates, nut butters and oats supply a hefty helping of protein and fiber.

For energy balls, simple combinations of a binder, mix-ins and coatings let you whip up customized creations based on your tastes. Start with a base of peanut butter, almond butter, sunflower seed butter or tahini to bind ingredients. Add a liquid sweetener like maple syrup, agave or honey.

Then fold in a variety of mix-ins. Oats, nuts, seeds, coconut, cacao nibs, chocolate chips and dried fruit add flavor, texture and nutrients. Spices like cinnamon, coffee or vanilla further enhance taste.

After mixing and chilling the dough, roll into balls. Optional coatings take flavors up a notch. Dip or roll balls in shredded coconut, seeds, granola, cacao powder or nuts. The options are endless!

Basic template for making energy balls:

- 1 cup nut or seed butter
- 1/4 cup liquid sweetener
- 1 1/2 cups dry mix-ins
- 1/4 cup coatings or toppings

Easy mix-in options:

- Oats, almond meal, ground flax
- Nuts like almonds, walnuts, pecans

- Seeds like chia, sunflower, pumpkin

- Dried fruit - raisins, cranberries, apricots

- Coconut flakes, cacao nibs, chocolate chips

- Spices - cinnamon, espresso, vanilla

For grab-and-go convenience, energy bars follow a similar formula pressed into bars or slices. Start with a nut butter base along with sticky binders like dates, dried fruit or maple syrup to hold everything together.

Bulk up the bars with mix-ins like oats, puffed rice, seeds, nuts, coconut and chocolate chips or chunks. A touch of plant milk or oil helps bind if needed.

Pack the mixture into bars, chill thoroughly to set, then cut into squares or rectangles. Optional toppings like shredded coconut or chocolate drizzle dress them up.

Make a batch on weekends for ready-to-eat snacks all week long. Tweak flavors based on seasonal produce too - carrots and pumpkin in fall, berries in summer, etc.

Portable energy balls and bars supply long-lasting fuel for busy days thanks to fiber, protein and healthy fats. Satisfy sweet cravings on the go with these no-bake, customizable treats using simple wholesome ingredients.

Guilt-Free Vegan Desserts

You don't have to forgo sweets and treats when following a vegan diet. Plenty of plant-based desserts satisfy without the dairy, eggs and refined sugar. Discover delicious healthier alternatives to savor for an occasional guilt-free indulgence.

Nice Cream

Blend frozen bananas into soft serve "ice cream" texture. Mix in cocoa powder, peanut butter, berries or other ingredients for flavor. Rich in potassium and fiber. Customizable and kid-friendly.

Chocolate Avocado Pudding

Blend ripe avocado with cacao powder and sweeteners for creamy chocolate pudding. Avocados provide heart-healthy fats and creaminess without dairy. Top with fruit or toasted coconut.

Banana "Milkshakes"

Blend frozen banana and plant-based milk for thick, milkshake-like texture. Add your favorite flavors like peanut butter, berries, cocoa powder, cinnamon or vanilla.

Baked Apples

Core an apple, stuff with walnuts, raisins, cinnamon and bake until tender. Drizzle with maple syrup or cashew cream for a simple, cozy dessert.

Protein "Cookies"

Mix nut butter, protein powder, oats and nut milk into cookie dough. Scoop and bake for a high-protein treat. Play with mix-ins like cacao nibs, chocolate chips, nuts or dried fruit.

Chia Seed Pudding

Stir chia seeds into your choice of dairy-free milk. Refrigerate until thickened, about 1 hour. Top with fruit, coconut, granola or cacao nibs for texture.

No-Bake Energy Balls or Bars

Bind nut butter, oats, seeds, dried fruit and spices using dates. Form into balls or bars for grab-and-go sweets packed with nutrients and fiber.

Roasted Fruit

Roast sliced fruit like plums, peaches, pears or pineapple drizzled with maple syrup until caramelized. Enjoy alone or with coconut yogurt. Simple and delicious.

Dark Chocolate Trail Mix

Melt vegan chocolate chips with nut butter, then mix into nuts and dried fruit. Let set before eating for candy-like clusters that provide protein.

Sorbet or "Nice" Cream Bars

Purée frozen banana or other fruit into "ice cream," mix in nuts and dried fruit, then freeze in popsicle molds for homemade fruit bars.

You can still enjoy sweet treats without refined sugar or unhealthy fats. Satisfy cravings with wholesome plant-based swaps that delight your taste buds.

Smoothie Bowl Creations

Smoothie bowls make for fun and nutritious breakfasts or snacks. Blending up a fruit and veggie-packed base then topping with mix-ins creates an edible work of art bursting with nutrients. The possibilities for combinations are endless.

Nearly any blend of fruits, veggies and greens can become a smoothie bowl base. Banana, mango, pineapple, berries and citrus fruits provide sweetness. Kale, spinach, swiss chard, carrots and zucchini add nutrition. Liquid bases like almond milk, coconut water or orange juice blend everything smoothly.

Blend fruits and veggies of your choice until smooth and creamy. The consistency should be thick enough to mound in a bowl rather than drinking as a smoothie. Add a frozen banana if too thin.

Pour into a bowl and top decoratively with desired mix-ins. The toppings provide contrasting flavors and textures that make smoothie bowls fun.

Some nutritious add-ins to consider include:

- Sliced fruit - bananas, berries, mango, kiwi
- Diced avocado
- Nut butter - almond, peanut, sunflower seed
- Granola, toasted oats or muesli
- Nuts and seeds - chia, pumpkin, sunflower

- Dried fruit - raisins, cranberries, apricots
- Coconut flakes
- Nutritional yeast
- Cacao nibs or cacao powder

Use a combination of 3-5 toppings for visual appeal. Layer or arrange them artfully over the smoothie base. Let your creativity run wild!

Some enticing flavor combinations include:

- Tropical - Pineapple banana base with kiwi, coconut, chia seeds
- Berry - Mixed berry base with strawberries, granola, almond butter
- Green - Kale, banana, mango base with avocado, hemp seeds, cacao nibs
- Carrot Cake - Carrot, pineapple, cinnamon base with walnuts, raisins, coconut
- Chocolate - Cocoa, banana base with strawberries, cacao nibs, nut butter

Smoothie bowls make a perfect weekend breakfast when you have time to get creative. But simple muesli with nut milk also works for rushed weekday mornings.

Let seasons guide your produce choices too. In summer, load up on stone fruits and melons. Fall and winter offer pumpkin, sweet potato, apples and pears.

Incorporate supplements if desired for an extra boost - spirulina, maca, hemp, chlorella, and moringa powders blend easily.

With endless flavor options, smoothie bowls serve up beauty, nutrition and fun. Blend up your favorite fruits and vegetables, then let your creativity run wild topping these edible bowls of goodness!

Plant-Based Baking Basics

Baking without dairy and eggs allows you to enjoy cakes, cookies, muffins and more on a vegan diet. With a few substitutions, your favorite baked goods can be just as delicious. Understand these simple plant-based swaps.

Replace Eggs

Ground flax or chia seeds mixed with water mimic the binding properties of eggs. Use 1 tablespoon of ground seeds whisked with 3 tablespoons of water per egg in recipes. Applesauce and banana also add moisture and structure when baking. Commercial egg replacers made from starches or legumes work too.

Use Plant Milk

Non-dairy milks like almond, oat, soy or coconut substitute for cow's milk in baking recipes. Stick with unsweetened varieties. For richness, cashew cream adds creamy texture to frostings and fillings. When baking, opt for milks with higher fat content to replicate buttery richness.

Swap Butter

Non-hydrogenated vegan butter sticks mimic the fat and flavor of dairy butter. Coconut oil or vegetable oil blends also substitute in the same quantity. For extra moisture, add a few tablespoons of applesauce or plant milk when using oil instead of vegan butter.

Boost Flavor

Vanilla, cinnamon and spices like ginger, nutmeg or cardamom enhance flavor to make up for missing eggs. Citrus zest also brightens baked goods. When adapting recipes, feel free to bump up spice amounts.

Replace Honey

Maple syrup, agave or brown rice syrup substitute well for honey in baking. Use the same quantity, but these liquid sweeteners add extra moisture, so reduce other wet ingredients slightly. Granulated sugars like coconut sugar also replicate sweetness well.

Use Flax "Eggs"

Whisk 1 tablespoon of ground flax meal with 3 tablespoons of water and let sit for 5 minutes to gel. This egg replacement adds structure and moisture to baked goods. Adjust consistency with more or less water.

Swap Greek Yogurt

Silken tofu pureed in a blender mimics the texture of Greek yogurt in baking recipes. The protein content also helps bind and create structure. For flavor, stir in lemon juice and vanilla.

Mind the Chemistry

Since plant-based ingredients behave differently, don't drastically alter baking recipes. Stick to direct substitute swaps, and make small adjustments as needed based on texture and moisture. Allow for adjustments during your first try.

Have fun exploring plant-based baking and finding new favorite sweets and treats without dairy or eggs. A few simple substitutions transform traditional recipes into vegan delights the whole family can enjoy.

Lane Payne

BONUS 1

AUDIOBOOK

Scan the QR code and listen to the audiobook

Lane Payne

BONUS 2

VIDEO

Scan the QR code

Lane Payne

EXCLUSIVE BONUS

3 EBOOK

Scan the QR code or click the link and access the bonuses

http://subscribepage.io/01tYl3

Lane Payne

AUTHOR BIO
LANE PAYNE

Lane's journey into the world of plant-powered living is rooted in a rich tapestry of experiences, making them a trusted guide for those seeking a sustainable and delicious vegan lifestyle.

Lane's exploration of plant-based living began as a personal quest for a healthier and more environmentally conscious way of life. Drawing from a background in nutritional sciences, Lane seamlessly combines expertise with a passion for creating meals that are not only wholesome but also budget-friendly, catering to individuals looking to embrace a healthy vegan lifestyle without breaking the bank.

By day, Lane emerges as a culinary enthusiast, experimenting with flavors and ingredients to craft plant-based meals that tantalize taste buds while nourishing the body. This hands-on approach, combined with a commitment to sustainability, forms the backbone of Lane's philosophy—the belief that a plant-based diet can be both accessible and delectable.

Lane Payne is not just an author; they are a champion of the plant-based movement, fostering a community of individuals eager to embrace a healthier, planet-friendly lifestyle.

Lane Payne

Printed in Great Britain
by Amazon